JOURNEY TO SIGHT

SEEING BEYOND THE NATURAL

H.S. JACKSON

Journey to Sight

© 2025 by Haseena Shaheed-Jackson

All rights reserved. No portion of this publication may be reproduced, stored in a retrieval system, or transmitted by any means—electronic, mechanical, photocopying, recording, or any other—except for brief quotations in printed reviews, without the prior written permission of the publisher.

Library of Congress Control Number: 2025907482
ISBN: 978-1-964686-51-6 (paperback) 978-1-964686-52-3 (ebook)

This book is based on true events reflecting the author's memory of them. Some names and characteristics may have been changed, some events compressed, and some dialogue recreated.

All Bible passages referenced in this book are taken from the New International Version unless otherwise indicated.

Editors: Jennifer Casey, Abby Dengler, Kim O Morgen
Cover and Interior Design: Emma Elzinga

Printed in the United States of America

First Edition

3 West Garden Street, Ste. 718
Pensacola, FL 32502
www.indigoriverpublishing.com

Ordering Information:

Quantity sales: Special discounts are available on quantity purchases by corporations, associations, and others. For details, contact the publisher at the address above.

Orders by US trade bookstores and wholesalers: Please contact the publisher at the address above.

With Indigo River Publishing, you can always expect great books, strong voices, and meaningful messages. Most importantly, you'll always find . . . *words worth reading.*

CONTENTS

Introduction 1

Chapter 1: See Beyond the Environment 13
    My Systems 15
    The Analysis 22

Chapter 2: See the Potential 27
    There Is More 30
    Potential 35

Chapter 3: The Plan 39
    Complete the Equation 42
    All About Me 49
    Ask Him 52

Chapter 4: The Way to the Plan 57
    Get Through the Desert 60
    Not Survive but Thrive 61
    Finding Purpose 65

Chapter 5: Detour Adds to Character 75
    See In the Word 79
    Make That Move 80
    Action is Required 81
    See the Rock 85

Chapter 6: See Hope and a Future 89
    The Lesson 91
    Fresh Start 93

    I Am Complete 97
    Lessons From the Detour 99

Chapter 7: Visualize the Journey 105
    Reflect On the Lessons 110
    Sharpening 115
    Embrace the Journey 117

Chapter 8: See in the Quiet Place 121
    See the Hidden Treasure 125
    See as God Sees 126

Chapter 9: See the Transition 131
    See to Move. 133
    Follow the Vision 134
    One More Thing 136
    Shed the Baggage. 139
    Seeing the Wrong Way. 142

Chapter 10: Evict Unbelief. 147
    Help My Unbelief. 150
    Overthinking 156
    See Past Fear 159

Chapter 11: See Yourself. 173
    Epilogue. 183
    Spirit Does Not Give Up. 184
    See to Transform. 186

Questions for Reflection. 191

INTRODUCTION

'What no eye has seen, no ear has heard, and what no human heart has conceived'—the things God has prepared for those who love him.

– 1 Corinthians 2:9

There is a plan for your life that you cannot see—a plan that is predestined just for you. You must believe in what is not presently visible, trusting in the Spirit to be your guide. It is through the Spirit that you will discover and live in your purpose. The Spirit is your guide and counselor to living a life of true wellness, joy, and fulfillment. What you will receive from God is outside of the world's control. What is for you cannot be understood by anyone but you; however, the Spirit sees and knows all.

Physical sight is a blessing. It allows us to witness God's creation and the wonders of nature: trees, animals, and streams. With it, you can take in the dawn of each new day and the fall of each sunset. You can watch your children grow and experience the many artistic pleasures of this world.

However, even some people who are physically blind may still be able to see. Since they have broken their dependence on earthly vision, they have trained themselves to see with the Spirit. The Spirit is the force which gives you power and strength, feeds us with positive energy and vibrations, and gives insight when making decisions that incorporate your values and beliefs. The Spirit enables us to be at peace in a world of chaos—it keeps you calmly centered and says, "Follow me, all is well."

Following the Spirit is vital to obtaining completeness and wholeness. To experience completeness requires the harmony of mind, body, and spirit. These three elements work together, helping us live a more successful existence. It is the Spirit that enables you to see past the dead ends that others see. And when you think you cannot go any farther, it says, "Keep going."

This place of relying on the Spirit is where I wanted and needed to be to find balance and harmony in my life. I wanted the sight that would motivate, inspire, drive me to go farther, and strive for the "more" beyond my natural sight. The "more" is living my best in all aspects of my life. Living my best does not mean that I have a ten rating in all spheres. Rather, it means living to maximize the potential in all areas of life in alignment to the purpose of one's life. I desired to maximize my health and well-being, with high levels of wellness, making conscious choices fueled by love, meaning, and purpose. I wanted to believe in what could not be seen and have faith that, ultimately, all would become visible. I had to look beyond my current circumstances to see what I needed to learn, using the type of sight that truly mattered.

In all the jobs I worked, I never fit in. Historically, I would work a job for no more than five years before moving on. Even in the job I worked at for twenty years, I was unfulfilled. There was always a restlessness within me that something was missing.

I was a renegade, never conforming to the mindsets of those around me that were content to stay idle. I was not willing to settle for a job that only paid my bills, put food on my table, and provided a roof over my head. I wanted more. I knew that there was something better for me in my future. My restlessness did not allow me to plant roots. It made me hunger to do more and be more by serving God. Romans 12:2 states, "Do not conform to the pattern of this world, but be transformed by the renewing of your mind." I had a thirst for this continual renewal and development, not for conforming and being confined. I wanted to be free.

I came to discover what this means: breaking from the molds imposed by society, culture, and even our own limiting beliefs. It means challenging the status quo and embracing a mindset that transcends mere conformity. Instead of passively adhering to the norms dictated by external forces, you are called to actively engage in the process of renewal—a transformation that originates from within.

As I let this verse transform my life, I uncovered seven crucial steps to achieve this internal change:

1. Embrace critical thinking: Question assumptions, challenge conventional wisdom, and seek understanding beyond surface-level knowledge. Develop a habit of examining ideas from multiple perspectives, and foster a deeper understanding of the world.

2. Cultivate self-awareness: Take time for introspection and recognize how your thoughts and actions are influenced by external factors. Strive for authenticity in belief and behavior. Understand personal values, strengths, and weaknesses.

3. Practice mindfulness: Train the mind to be present in the moment—free from distractions and judgments. This allows you to observe your thoughts and emotions without attachment, fostering greater clarity and emotional resilience.

4. Actively pursue growth opportunities: Embrace challenges as opportunities for learning. Step out of your comfort zone, try new experiences, and seek personal development initiatives that expand your perspective and capabilities.

5. Nurture positive relationships: Surround yourself with individuals who inspire and support your journey of transformation. Engage in meaningful conversations, exchange ideas, and learn from diverse viewpoints.

6. Cultivate gratitude: Shift focus away from what you lack, and appreciate the blessings and opportunities already present in your life.

7. Align with purpose: Discover passion in life. Align your thoughts and actions with meaningful goals that resonate with your personal values and aspirations.

Transforming the mind is a continuous journey of growth, self-discovery, and conscious evolution. It requires courage to challenge the familiar, resilience to overcome obstacles, and commitment to embrace change. As you renew your mind, you not only transcend the patterns of this world but also become an agent of transformation, inspiring others to embark on their own journey of self-discovery and renewal.

For me, this process required taking a leap and being uncomfortable in order to create the future and life that fulfilled me. I knew it was possible, even though it would require sacrifice, courage, and dedication: sacrifice because I would have to give up being comfortable with a steady, financially stable job in order to pursue my desire to be an entrepreneur; courage because I would have to connect with individuals and take on roles I would not have considered possible in the past; dedication because I would have to put in the time and effort to reach my goals.

Within every person are two competing forces. The first force clings to safety and attempts to minimize fear, and the second force yearns for wholeness and completion by being true to oneself. It is the second force that I wanted to control my life. I had a deep desire to not just live, but to be impactful and make a difference by helping others. I had gone as far as I could in my job. Now it was time for my career. I wanted to partner with others to support them in their journey for more, as I had done.

In my career, I wanted to help individuals know true joy, not just happiness. Happiness is typically associated with a sense of well-being and satisfaction—a symptom of circumstance. Joy, on the other hand, is a deep, enduring state of being. It produces a profound sense of contentment and inner peace. Unlike happiness, joy is not dependent on external circumstances but is instead related to our state of mind. It is a mindset that can persist even in the face of adversity. Joy is leaning into the Spirit to see beyond natural sight, yield the outcomes we desire, and help others focus on their own Spirit-empowered vision.

The Spirit is not fixated on the tangible, only on the intangible. It enables you to see and feel from a different perspective. You are not bound to clothes, jewelry, or money—items that come and go. Instead, your faith will provide for your basic needs, such as food and shelter. These will be provided because you are in alignment with your purpose. When you do the work that you were created to do, you will never lack. In fact, abundance is all around you. Just close your eyes and open your mind. Center your attention on being blessed; blessings will open doors that you believe are closed.

As you focus your mind on the resources you need, those resources are what you will receive. Be centered in faith and believe. You will become magnetic and attract what you need. This posture frees you to be your best self—a self that is not focused on material wealth or pleasing others but on pleasing God, the one who created you. Join him in the work he is doing. Put your gift to use and help to better our world. Attracting what you need is not about what you can get but about how you can add value to others so that they, in turn, are empowered to do the same.

Relying totally on physical sight is shortsighted. It causes misconceptions and prejudices, effecting your perception of situations and people and limiting what you can do. Because physical sight is so limited, we need spiritual sight to truly see. Spiritual sight enables us to remove limitations. The Spirit empowers us to see with hope and faith. As hope and faith grow, we will respond with actions that lead to flourishing instead of surviving.

As a child, my eyes controlled my life. Ultimately, my mother and father were great parents because they provided a solid foundation for their children. Specifically, they instilled in me a bedrock of faith and belief in who I am. They instilled in me that I am a person of value, so I do not allow any person to devalue me.

Even so, parts of what I witnessed and experienced initially placed limits on my potential. My mother worked for a brief period but suddenly stopped. I did not see her seeking out new employment or pursuing entrepreneurship. She was content with being a housewife. I am sure this was a joint decision by my parents. My father was the provider for the home. He valued hard work and dedication—values that became instilled in me. Our household had sufficient funds to maintain the essentials. But there were no remaining funds for recreational activities or for us children to explore our passions, attend summer camps, or travel. Both of my parents were content with sustaining a household on one salary that enabled us to survive but not thrive. There was no plan for a better future, so I believed one was not possible.

My parents were laborers: hardworking, dedicated to being independent, and not looking for handouts. As such, they instilled in their children that we must become laborers. While I appreciated the work ethic they gave me, this expectation also placed limitations on what we believed we could become. At the age of thirteen, when I entered high school, I aspired only to graduate and pursue a trade. There was no thought of going to college. Breaking free from the limitations of my environment opened a door, empowering me to see with the Spirit. This allowed me to go to college and eventually become a consultant and entrepreneur. It allowed me to take control of my story and become the author.

I had to learn that the limits I saw in my childhood were not final—that physical sight was blocking me from embracing and pursuing purpose. I learned that I could not allow my environment and the people in it to dictate my aspirations. Where I began did not have to control where I could go.

I eventually came to appreciate how my parents surpassed their own limits, too. My parents migrated from the South to escape racism and segregation in hopes of seeking a better life. Living in the South, Blacks were believed to be inferior. But my parents did not allow the words spoken by closed-minded and biased strangers to be their reality. The words my parents spoke were the opposite. They spoke, "I am somebody." They were somebody: people of beauty and power. This belief enabled them to survive and love the people that God created. What they spoke and reflected upon is what became their reality.

Unfortunately, total reliance on earthly vision is prevalent in the world today. Individuals allow their environment to place limits on their growth and potential. Our communities have great influence over our lives and lock us into the communal perspective, preventing us from discovering what we can do and who we can be.

We must be willing to change our community and keep moving forward. It saddens and angers me when people give their personal control to others. It saddens me because they are giving up on themselves and the chance for a life with possibility. It angers me because giving up is really complacency. It means accepting what life dishes out instead of seizing opportunities and creating a life that resonates with the Spirit. Time, effort, and dedication are the only ways to change the story.

A great example of this is the movie *Roadhouse*, starring Patrick Swayze. Swayze played John Dalton, a man who traveled the country changing the culture of nightclubs. John transformed clubs from unsavory establishments into attractive and welcoming businesses that were viable and sustainable. The movie centered on a club owner, Frank Tilghman, who operated in a town that was under the influence of a bully, Brad Wesley. Tilghman had a vision for his club, a vision he believed could become a reality. For the vision to be realized, it would take courage, grit, and perseverance. Tilghman did not allow his environment and its people to control what he could see. He believed in his dream. He experienced major trials and obstacles, but ultimately, Tilghman's vision came to life. This movie summarizes how one can see beyond their physical sight and instead see with the Spirit.

This is what I had to learn to do—to see beyond my present situations and circumstances. I had to be like Tilghman and believe in the vision I had for my life, even as a small child. As a child, I had playtime with one of my cousins. I shared with her my dream to be a lawyer or a business executive, even though I did not really believe this was possible. I saw it as an opportunity to pretend, even without real hope. I saw my parents and my environment as barriers that I could not overcome. My mindset was "if" instead of "can."

In Mark 9:14–23, a father seeks healing for his son. The disciples do not help, and the father becomes discouraged. In verse 22, he says to Jesus, "But if you can do anything, take pity on us and help us."

Jesus replies, "'If you can?' Everything is possible for one who believes."

The father had an "if" attitude, contemplating the obstacles. Jesus had a "can" mindset, focused on possibilities.

In navigating life's challenges, adopting an "if" versus a "can" attitude profoundly influences outcomes. The "if" mentality fixates on uncertainties, dwelling on potential barriers and setbacks. This attitude yields hesitation, indecision, and missed opportunities. It breeds doubt. Individuals with an "if" mindset may find themselves paralyzed by the fear of potential failures. They might dwell excessively on what could go wrong, which can inhibit progress and personal growth. Additionally, an "if" attitude may contribute to a negative outlook, limiting creativity and innovation. Overall, the results of an "if" attitude include missed chances for success, reduced self-confidence, and a lack of fulfillment due to the reluctance to take risks and pursue goals wholeheartedly.

A "can" attitude, on the other hand, embodies optimism and resilience, allowing us to concentrate on solutions and ignite the drive to overcome. By adopting a "can" mindset, individuals unlock their full potential, paving the way for personal fulfillment, professional success, and a more enriching life journey. Embracing a "can" attitude cultivates a mindset of empowerment and self-belief. It fosters a willingness to innovate and persist in the face of adversity. Those with a "can" mentality tend to approach challenges as opportunities for growth, learning, and development. They harness their inner resources and external support networks to navigate complexities with resilience and grace. One transforms potential obstacles into steppingstones to success. A "can" mindset turns potential into reality.

As I looked at my community and its barriers, I had to adopt a "can" mindset to break free of my environment and become the person I was meant to be.

As I progressed on my journey to see, there were still lessons to learn. I made decisions based on my own sight that resulted in hardship and pain. When my brother passed, I turned to man instead of looking to the One who created me. However, turning to man eventually led me to look deep within myself—and to my creator—and see not with my eyes but with hope, faith, and the power of thinking. We are to see through these, not from the perspective of self but the perspective of God.

Every person has choices and options. It is up to the individual to identify and understand what those are. We will always encounter situations and circumstances that break us. But we must be broken to be made whole and see from God's perspective instead of our own. We are all the same. We all bleed and die. No one person can say they are better or more important than another person. If a person does have this perspective, it is a false reality. Their perspective is clouded by selfishness, pride, and insecurities. God's perspective allows us to shed our negative mindset and remove the "scales" that blind us. Once they are removed, we can see beyond physical sight.

See and enjoy the beauty of the world. Be thankful for the life you have been gifted. Strive to make the most of your life. Be impactful and make a difference by uplifting those around you. Help others to be their best instead of just settling for whatever life throws at them. Help them achieve the exhortation of Ephesians 4:22–24, which says to "put off your old self, which is being corrupted by its deceitful desires; to be made new in the attitude of your minds; and to put on the new self, created to be like God in true righteousness and holiness."

Seeing with the Spirit will enable you to change your world. It has changed mine, guiding me to see people and situations from a new perspective. As a result, it has transformed me into a better version of myself, someone who strives to be of value to others.

Before I learned this, I was so focused on what I could physically see that I was missing the beauty of my journey. My journey had missteps and failed attempts that caused me to think I was defeated, having to settle for whatever came my way. In one of my jobs, for example, I had seven different supervisors. Each one was progressively worse. I did not believe this was possible. I would think I had hit rock bottom with one supervisor, then the next would be even worse. I had to learn that it was not the supervisors who needed to change, but me.

My focus on physical sight caused me to only see my immediate environment, missing the lessons. Each supervisor taught me a lesson. Each helped me in my journey to grow, develop, and transform. I was so fixated on each supervisor's qualities that I failed to look within myself, to see what the Spirit was leading me to do. I had to see beyond my environment to shift my focus within and make the intangible become tangible. I had to seek understanding and gain wisdom to aid me in moving forward instead of lamenting and becoming complacent. I had to learn that circumstances occur for a reason. It is up to us to look beneath the surface—to find and uncover their lessons.

In this book, I share my journey to sight so that each reader may find their own. Spiritual sight requires that you go deeper within, to see the world not with your eyes but with hope, joy, and love. Do not see with jaded perceptions and biases. Remove these barriers and discover the pathways to resolution. Find solutions through empowerment and self-responsibility. You are in control of yourself—what you think, believe, feel, and do. You are in control of living a life that is whole and complete.

Chapter 1
SEE BEYOND THE ENVIRONMENT

Clarity is the moment we see without opening our eyes.
– STEPHANIE BANKS, A SOULFUL AWAKENING

Our deepest moments of clarity don't come from what we physically see but from what we understand with our hearts, minds, and spirits. When we learn to trust our inner knowing, we recognize that true clarity often comes from within. But that understanding is a developmental process that must start somewhere.

Where you start is merely that—the start. Think about the runners in a race. Everyone starts at the beginning. However, each runner's journey will not be the same. Each will get to the finish line in their own time, using stamina and endurance. These factors will determine how they run their individual race with their individual gifts.

The start of the race is determined by our environment and social systems: family, friends, neighborhoods, cultures, school systems, etc. In the human services profession, one of the methods used to evaluate and understand individuals is the General Systems Theory. This theory states that various elements in an individual's environment mold their thoughts, attitudes, beliefs, and behaviors. These elements are the systems that play a vital role in the development of one's sense of identity. Analyzing an individual's systems allows one to look at an individual holistically.

The systems of an individual can hinder growth because of barriers created by one's culture and experiences. The barriers impact our mindset and can cause us to settle in life. It takes willpower to make change in those systems, to break away and run the race of life. This is what I had to do to break through the ceiling that my environment had constructed over my life.

My mom had me at almost fifty years old. Because of her age, she lacked patience and could not relate to me. She would call me stupid when she became angry or upset with something I did. Because of this, I believed I must be stupid. I know she did not call me these names maliciously. It was merely her way of expressing her anger. Still, I had to break through this barrier of believing myself to be inferior and reprogram my mind toward a different narrative.

Think of Cinderella as another example. Her systems—that is, her stepmother and stepsisters—impacted her mindset and beliefs. Cinderella had to break through the barriers of her environment to see that she could be a princess, not a servant to her evil stepmother and sisters. It took her fairy godmother to break her out of prison and open her eyes to see. The analogy speaks to how one must open their mind to see beyond their systems that place barriers and constraints on them. Unfortunately, I have encountered a few Cinderellas who could not break through these barriers. They gave up on becoming the person that existed inside of them waiting to break free.

My Systems

Family

Family lays the foundation for values and beliefs. A baby looks to the mother for safety and security. The bond that forms between mother and child enables the child to be confident. Rooted in this bond, the child will be able to adapt and recover from trials as well as establish healthy relationships. The bond influences how the child's perspective and mindset will develop—whether the child will be calm and resilient or fearful and anxious about how to exist in the world.

My family was the first system that shaped what I thought I could accomplish in life. My experiences in this system impacted what I saw and believed, effecting my aspirations and mindset. Both of my parents migrated from the South to Illinois to seek a better life. They did create a better life for themselves and their children, and because of them, our household did not have to experience the racism and segregation of the South. My father served in the Vietnam War before meeting and marrying my mom. They created a home that was safe and comfortable. However, being comfortable can cause you to settle and become complacent—following the security of what is known and minimizing the unknown out of fear, even though it is the unknown that results in growth and evolution. This is the mindset that was passed on to me.

Being comfortable means making enough money to keep food on the table, clothes on your back, and a roof over your head. However, there was no drive to be anything more than average or do anything more than just to get by. Their philosophy on life was reflected by their shopping habits. My family would go to the mall to shop for clothes twice a year: once for the winter and once for school clothes. I had four or five pairs of shoes to sustain me for the year. There was no need for more. There was no thought of going beyond that. The goal was to maintain in every way.

Obtaining funds for programs and activities that would enable us to grow was not an option. My parents did not enroll me in after school programs to broaden my education and skills or aid in my development. Instead, I just lived. I went to school and came home. There were no extracurricular activities. My parents had no aspirations to generate wealth to add value to their children's experiences. There was no drive to be more than just average.

I believe it is the parents' responsibility to challenge their child to become better than themselves. A parent is the most influential person in the child's life. Therefore, the parent has the power to speak life into the child and should inspire the child to become greater and better; I received no such encouragement.

Initially, my mom worked; however, she lost her job and did not return to the workforce. She became a full-time stay-at-home-mom. Her philosophy, which was the foundation of her culture, was that women should be content with raising a family and managing the household. There was no need to pursue education or to have a career. She also never learned to drive a car, always dependent upon my dad or friends for transportation. Her mobility limited what she could do, but her mind was closed to other possibilities. She placed a ceiling on the growth in her life.

Just as culture had placed limits on her thinking, she placed those limitations on her daughters. She trained me using what worked for her. I was to find a husband who could make me a home. This mindset worked well in her day and era; however, the world was evolving, and women were taking on more roles in society. Women were landing higher paying jobs and making strides in the business world beyond being a secretary or receptionist.

The limiting mindset of my mom did not make her a bad person. She did the best that she could with what she knew, but her way of thinking was shaped by the circumstances she grew up in. Culture shapes our expectations of gender roles. Women have historically been oppressed, harassed, and denied education while men are men were given free reign and access to all.

However, God created both male and female in his image to be imitators of Christ. We are one humanity, distinct by our gender, each with a role to play in this world. Men and women can both work and be included in leadership roles. In Galatians 3:28, the Apostle Paul explains that all are new in Christ—there is no distinction based on race, ethnicity, class, gender, or any physical characteristic. It is clear that every person matters to God. Afterall, God created man and woman to be a team, not to be adversaries or for one to be superior.

Love is the key to combating limited thinking. Loving God and oneself removes the barriers that place limits one's value. Women must love themselves, not looking to anything or anyone else to define who they are except God.

In addition to my mom and dad, I was fortunate to have my

grandmother live in our household for a few years of my life. My mom and her three sisters banded together and took turns providing a home for her. She had lived in Louisiana in a small town called El Dorado for as long as she could, until her health began failing and her finances were depleted. My grandfather passed away before I was born, so my grandma needed support.

I loved my "Grandme." That was my nickname for her. "Grandme" meant she was the grandmother for me. She made me feel special because she made a point of keeping me around her. Wherever she went, I was in tow. Grandme stayed with us in Chicago during the summer, spring, and fall. She traveled to California to stay with my aunt for the winter when it was hard to get around in the snow and the Chicago weather aggravated her arthritis.

Whenever she stayed with us, I would spend the entire day with her. We had a routine. We would get up in the morning, eat breakfast, then watch our favorite soap opera, *The Young and Restless*, followed by lunch. Grandme often made me grilled cheese sandwiches. Those were my favorite. She used that gooey cheese that would melt in your mouth. When I pulled the sandwich apart, the cheese would be like a rubber band, thick and rich in flavor. After lunch, we would continue watching TV. I was just happy being with Grandme.

As with most children, my family was my entire world. They were my role models. My mom and grandmother were both happy and content in their roles, so I felt this was surely the path for me to follow.

FAITH

My father was raised in the Catholic Church, which is where I began my journey in religion. My family attended a local church that was within walking distance from our home. My mother and father believed in the Lord and instilled this belief in me as a child.

Not only did my parents teach me about God, but so did my Grandme, who was a Baptist. On some Sundays, I attended the Baptist church on the corner with Grandme. Although I did not understand what was going on, I enjoyed the singing and all the clapping, dancing, and stomping that came with it. People stood in front of pews and filled the aisles. I sat in the pew next to Grandme, happy and content to just be in her company at church, enjoying the songs and music.

What I most clearly recall is that the atmospheres of the Catholic and Baptist churches were totally different. The Catholic services lacked enthusiasm and life. The songs were not lively like in the Baptist church. I would leave church with my Grandme singing and dancing.

Even though we did not join the Baptist church and I wasn't baptized there, it had a great influence on me. My Grandme supported my parents by teaching me about faith and worship, instilling Christian values in me, and giving me a strong spiritual foundation. As I reflect, I am happy that my parents were not closed-minded about me learning different faith traditions. They were not stuck in one rigid mindset where the household would only follow and support Catholicism. This openness created a new spiritual pathway of growth for the family.

One day, my father came home excited, telling my mom that he had a new place for us to attend church. Just like the Beverly Hillbillies, we piled into the car the next Sunday morning on a new adventure. Thus, my journey into Islam began.

The Bible states that the man is the head of the household, and the wife is to obediently follow his decisions. If the man is a believer, he sets the tone for the household. Dad believed in God. Even though I was too young to understand why we changed religions at the time, I can look back and see that he was trying to find his way and take his family with him. He saw Islam as the way.

Each Sunday, we arrived at the mosque at 10 a.m. and would stay until around 3 or 4 p.m. Immediately upon arriving, the men and women went separate directions because the congregation was segregated by sex. The mosque we attended had three levels: the main floor, the balcony, and the basement. My brother would go with my dad to sit on the main level in the front. My sister and I would follow my mom to sit either on the main level at the back of the room—or in the balcony if we couldn't sit still. The basement is where the women who had infants would sit. An imaginary dividing line ran between the men and women.

Each week, we would arrive at the mosque, go to our seats, and be quiet. After about an hour, it became torture. At about 1 p.m., my stomach would begin rumbling from hunger. My mom would bring some crackers for us to snack on to keep us quiet, but this was not enough for me. I wanted some food. Sitting quietly without food or play for seven hours was too much for me. I looked forward to Sundays as if I was walking to the guillotine.

At each service, there would be a lineup of speakers for the day. The speakers would be leaders in the Islamic community. I do not recall who they were or what they talked about. I was too young to comprehend, and I did not ask questions of my parents. I just recall the order of the services. The speakers would speak, then the Imam would wrap up the service. Once he got to talking, I was more than ready to go home. I would think that by the time it was the Imam's turn to talk, he would understand he needed to be brief. I would also think that the Iman was hungry. I know that other kids felt the same as I did. They were getting antsy and were ready to go. There is only so much talking that people can take in a day.

Each speaker was long-winded. It is because of these speakers that I believe one should get to the point when speaking. People like brevity and simplicity—concepts the leaders in the mosque seemed unfamiliar with. They would talk and talk and talk. I was not inspired or motivated to attend the mosque. One day, I told my mother this. I got the worst spanking of my life. Needless to say, I did not voice this opinion again. I suffered going to the mosque in silence.

One day, things changed. I do not recall the reason why. Our Imam was Elijah Muhammad, and his son, Wallace Dee Muhammad, was to be his predecessor. But in this transition of roles, something happened that caused many of the followers to fall away. The mosque was then taken over by Louis Farrakhan. All I know is that when Louis Farrakhan became the Imam, we stopped attending.

I went from attending mosque every Sunday to not going to services at all. Suddenly, my wish had finally come true. My nightmare of having to attend the mosque every Sunday had come to an end. I was elated. My parents did not seek out another church or mosque, so this was my last encounter with a religion in childhood.

Religion should be the choice of every individual. Religion is not a dictatorship. Every person is to find their way. By forcing a faith on a person, you are taking away their independence and autonomy. Independence and autonomy are vital for a person to form their own identity.

Even though we stopped attending the mosque, my mom was

faithful and dedicated to reading the Quran daily. I have memories of her sitting at the table reading. That spurred my passion for reading—not the Quran, which I have never read—but for reading mysteries and Harlequin romances. I had a thirst for reading and would go through a book in one to two days.

I recall always being restless. I would get bored doing the same thing, bored with the same routine. I always wanted to do something new and different. My mom would get exasperated with me because she did not understand that I wanted more. Reading was my avenue of escape. Escaping the boredom of my life. I dreamed of being like the characters in my book. These women were independent. These women were business executives and leaders in their community. Reading was my way of seeing a different life than the one I lived.

After school, I would go to my room to read for the rest of the day. On weeknights, I had to force myself to stop reading by 10 or 11 p.m. But on weekends, I would read until the wee hours of the morning. The sun would be rising by the time I would stop reading. I would think to myself, "Wow, it is a new day." When I read, time did not matter. I was in another world, lost in the pleasure of reading.

THE ANALYSIS

My family and culture laid the groundwork for the person I would become. My environment placed limits on my aspirations. Popular biblical teachings assign roles in which wives are nurturers and husbands are breadwinners.[1] These biblical teachings were the

---

1   Katelyn Beaty, "Women's work is in the home—and out of it" in *Cultural Engagement: A Crash Course in Contemporary Issues* by Joshua D. Chatraw and Karen Swallow Prior, (Zondervan Academic, 2019), 119–122.

foundation of my household. These systems threatened to place me in a mold.

Because of this foundation, I had a yearning for more. I knew there was a better life where men and women could coexist, being co-laborers and co-leaders. I sought to change the paradigm for myself, rethinking the dichotomy. I was determined to break the mold in my family. I was not going to conform; I would pave a new path, showing my parents and siblings that we could be more. And as I continued reading on the topic, I discovered more voices advocating for the idea that women do not have to leave behind womanhood to glorify God through working.[2] We do not need to leave behind being a woman to pursue freedom and independence.

Despite some of the limiting effects of my culture, my parents and grandmother did give me a spiritual foundation, and my mom instilled in me the passion of reading. Watching my mom read, I learned how to feed my faith. My parents also taught me to value myself. They taught me that I was not inferior; I should speak up and not back down.

In eighth grade, I had an altercation with my teacher. We had an argument in the classroom in front of all my classmates. I spoke my mind. My teacher did not like what I said, so she had me removed from her class. My parents had to come meet with the principal. I was placed in another eighth-grade class to finish the remainder of the school year. After the meeting, my mom and dad told me that I should always stand up for myself, but I was wrong in being disrespectful. There was a better way I could have handled the issue.

---

2   Owen Strachan, "The beauty of centering life around the home: A complementarian perspective of women and work" in *Cultural Engagement*, Chatraw and Prior, 118.

This encounter had a lasting impact on me. Later in my life, I analyzed this incident to get clarity on what made me act out. I do not recall the specifics. What I do recall is that I felt devalued. I felt the teacher was being demeaning. I understood then that being respected is one of my non-negotiable values. All people matter and deserve to be treated fairly. No person has the right to treat another person as less-than. I have built upon this foundation.

My family and culture provided my starting point toward forging a better way of life for myself. I felt a strong pull to see beyond the systems of my childhood. If I had remained in those systems, I would have been giving up on what was within me. I was only at the beginning of my life. I had yet to uncover my purpose and the value I would add to this world. But one thing I knew was that I was not going to settle for just being good; I had to strive to be excellent. This would require me to take a deep look within myself and beyond what I could see to create my vision. I owed it to myself to break out of my environment and feed my hunger for *more*.

To me, "more" means striving to leave a legacy. Legacy is often misconstrued as a sum of possessions or achievements left behind by those who have departed. However, true legacy transcends material wealth or accolades; it resides in the intangible imprints left within the hearts and minds of those who remain. It is about the values, beliefs, and memories that shape who you are and how you impact the world around you.

Living out the legacy that resides within you is paramount. It is a conscious choice to embrace the wisdom, love, and guidance passed down to you by your predecessors. My predecessors are my mom, dad, and Grandme. My mission is to internalize their teachings and carry forward the torch of their virtues in my daily life to build a better future.

Living out your legacy honors the past while embracing the present and future. It is about fostering connections that build bridges of empathy, compassion, and understanding, rather than walls of division. It means leaving a positive imprint on the world by embodying the principles passed down through generations.

Living the legacy within you entails a commitment to continuous growth and self-reflection. It requires you to be mindful of your actions and choices, recognizing their ripple effects on others. By embodying the virtues and principles instilled in you, you become a steward of a legacy that transcends time and space.

Ultimately, your legacy is not about what you leave behind, but what endures within you. It serves as a reminder to cherish the memories, lessons, and values bestowed upon you and to carry them forward with purpose and integrity. By doing so, you not only honor the legacy of those who came before you but also pave the way for a brighter and more compassionate future.

I want to leave behind a legacy of kindness, empathy, and resilience—a legacy that inspires others to carry the torch forward and make a positive difference in the world. I am embracing the legacy that is within me, striving to be the embodiment of its enduring spirit.

Chapter 2

SEE THE POTENTIAL

Believe in your infinite potential. Your only limitations are those you set upon yourself.

— Roy T. Bennett, The Light in the Heart

Potential is your personal power that propels you to strive for more. One must grow to understand and utilize this power. However, as the baby of the litter, I placed limits on my potential by following my family members—especially my siblings.

I grew up with "Follow Me Syndrome," meaning that I latched onto others in my household. First, I latched on to Grandme. When she moved away, I attached myself to my brother and sister. As the baby of the family, I guess that is what you do: you follow others for companionship. This desire is natural; at our core, humans are inherently social creatures, drawing strength and meaning from our connections with others. Especially as a child, it is through these vital relationships and shared experiences that we grow and find fulfillment. God did not intend for a person to walk through life in solitude but to thrive by embracing community. But when you're the youngest, your older siblings don't always see it that way.

There was a two-year age difference between me and my brother and a seven-year gap between me and my sister. Wherever they sought to go, I wanted to go with them. My sister would not let me tag along with her much. She was a teenager doing the normal things teens do. She had a boyfriend who she was gooey-eyed over, and she spent most of her time with him. I would have been a third and unwelcomed wheel. There were times when she took pity on me and allowed me to tag along. She knew that if she did not take me out with her, I would sit in the house for most of the day. It was not like I was in high demand with a full calendar of activities jockeying for my time.

When I was not able to tag along with my sister, I would latch on to my brother. I would tag along with him and his friends. My brother was my protector. He made sure no one bothered me or questioned me following along.

My parents had one rule: we had to play on the block within ear shot. My brother and I adhered to this rule of hanging out only on the block. When it was time to come home, my father would whistle by placing two of his fingers in his mouth. When he whistled, we were to run home immediately, or there would be consequences of a spanking or punishment—neither of which appealed to me.

Once I graduated from grammar school, I followed my brother to John Marshall Harlan High School. My sister had already graduated when I became a freshman, but my brother was only two grades above me. My brother instructed me to go into Home Economics to learn a trade, graduate, and get a job, just as he had been instructed by my sister. This was the plan for our lives. This was the only option in our household. Learn a trade to get a job. Both of my parents' highest level of education was high school, so my parents didn't expect or require anything more from us. We did not discuss visions or aspirations in our family.

My family members had no desire to get more out of life beyond meeting basic needs. My father was a homebody. Monday through Friday, my father had the same routine: wake up, get dressed, eat breakfast, go to work, come home, eat dinner. After eating dinner, he would sit in his favorite chair in the living room watching television for the rest of the day, then go to bed. He was like Archie Bunker.

My dad's mindset was that he had a great job working for Conrail. He had been employed with the company for over thirty years. He received a steady paycheck that sustained his household. He was a good example of what can happen with hard work and dedication while working for someone else. There is nothing wrong with working for someone else; the issue is giving up on becoming better and being more. My parents' focus in life was singular: survival.

Once he retired, there was a slight variation in my dad's schedule. Instead of being away from home for eight hours, he would leave the house daily after breakfast to run errands for a few hours, return to eat lunch, watch television, eat dinner, and then go to bed. He viewed retirement as "arriving." He had paid his dues and reached the pinnacle of his life. The time had come for him to enjoy the fruits of his labor—a pension. There was no need to generate more income. His focus was to survive—nothing more or less.

My parents' mindset was the product of where they started, having to survive and break away from an oppressive and racist environment. But once they landed in Illinois, they remained stuck in this mindset of surviving. Their driving force was safety and security. My parents did not level up in their thinking or reach to live out the full expression of their true selves. My parents did not see the need to strive for more.

My dad had overcome the fight to live rather than be killed due to racism. He escaped, found a good wife, and had a family. Having reached these goals, he stopped growing. Growing was frightening. To experience high levels of wellness and self-actualization, one must be willing to be uncomfortable. Wellness requires evolving in consciousness and being self-directed, resulting in achieving full potential.

My parents passed their way of thinking down to me. No one mentioned college. There were no discussions about the world being full of opportunities; no one asked what I wanted out of life or who I wanted to become. Imagining possibilities requires seeing beyond physical sight—seeing with the Spirit.

There Is More

In my freshman year of high school, I encountered the woman who would be my mentor for four years. She is the one who helped me change my thinking to believing—believing that I could make choices toward a more successful existence. That I could break through the limiting barriers of my environment, tap into my potential, and take responsibility for myself. That I could make decisions that would move me to higher levels of wellness, turning potential into reality.

My sister was a gym leader when she attended high school, and she pointed me in Ms. Davis's direction. She spoke highly of

Ms. Davis, so I signed up to be a gym leader where Ms. Davis was the coordinator.

Ms. Jane Davis was a woman small in stature but big in spirit and heart. She was petite at four feet, nine inches tall, with sandy brown hair. I always thought a stiff wind could blow her over. She had a strong, deep, raspy voice—probably a result of her smoking. You would not think a woman of her size could have such a strong and deep voice.

One day in gym class, Ms. Davis called me out with that formidable voice.

"Shaheed," she said, using my last name.

Oh boy, I thought, walking over to her.

"I see you walking home from school every day holding a folded piece of paper in your hand," she said. "Where are your books and your homework?"

I looked at her smugly. "I don't need my books. I finish my homework in class and on breaks."

"What's on the paper you carry?" she asked.

"The information I need to review," I replied. "I write it all down, so I don't have to carry my books back and forth."

She looked at me with shock.

She stated, "That is not acceptable. You are more than that."

I gave her a look, as if to say, "...and?"

Ms. Davis stated, "Tomorrow, you will meet me in the principal's office at 8 a.m."

I gasped, "WHAT?"

Nonetheless, I met her in the principal's office as directed, and this thirty-minute meeting changed my life. I do not recall the specifics of the meeting. What I do recall is that Ms. Davis took the time to make me feel valued. She talked to me about potential, purpose, and aspirations. She stated that limits were self-imposed and constructed. In fact, the world was wide open, full of opportunities and possibilities. It was up to me to take advantage of them. She told me I was to strive for better and not settle for what life dished out. I was to make my own decisions and not allow my environment to dictate what I could do or become. I needed to break out of my environment and the ceiling it constructed. This meeting opened my mind up to a different world and way of living. It was the first step to seeing beyond my physical sight.

This was a turning point for me. I went from walking home with a folded sheet of paper to carrying books and papers. I enrolled in honors classes. I was being challenged. I was on the path to "more." The lid that my environment placed on me had been blown off. I could see past what was in front of me. There was so much more than what I had seen.

As I look back, I see that God used my sister to move me in the direction that I needed to go. I was created for a purpose and a reason. If I had kept my mind closed, I would have missed out on His plans. I would not be fulfilling the purpose of my creation. Ms. Davis was the first guide on my journey.

This moment in my life reminds me of King David. He became a great leader because he lifted the lid that had been placed on his life by his family. His father saw him as nothing more than a keeper of sheep. In fact, he was to be a keeper—but of God's people rather than sheep.

Each person has some type of lid on their life. The key is what each individual will do with that lid. Will they allow the lid to keep them down, or will they break through?

David chose to break free. Like David, I also chose to break through. This enabled me to see possibilities. I had a gift that I needed to develop and utilize. I had to have faith and believe in making my vision a reality.

It was my responsibility to tap into my potential. I love my family dearly; however, their sight was limited. They saw what the world wanted them to see.

My parents' sight was limited just like that of the servant of Elisha. In 2 Kings 6, the king of Aram is enraged with Elisha. The king sends his army to surround Elisha in the city of Dothan. Elisha's servant looks out the window and is petrified. He is overwhelmed with fear, but Elisha sees beyond the immediate danger. He says to his servant, "Don't be afraid. Those who are with us are more than those who are with them." Elisha then prays, "Open his eyes, Lord, so that he may see." He is not asking for a literal change in the servant's physical eyesight but a spiritual revelation of God's presence and power. When the servant looks outside again, he sees with God's sight and finds hills full of God's army, ready to defend Elisha and his servant from the king's forces.

Elisha's response challenges us to consider the importance of spiritual sight versus physical sight. Physical sight, while essential for navigating the world, inherently imposes limitations on your perspective. The human eye has finite capabilities in terms of range, acuity, and depth perception. Your peripheral vision is less acute, and your focus is limited to what lies directly before you. These physical constraints influence how you perceive and interpret your surroundings.

Beyond physical sight lies a realm of broader cognitive and psychological factors that shape your perspective. Your past experiences, beliefs, and your cultural background all contribute to how you interpret what you see. This subjective lens means that two people can witness the same event yet perceive it differently based on their unique perspectives.

Elisha's perspective was deeply rooted in faith, belief, and hope in God's power. He saw beyond the immediate threat because his spiritual vision was guided by trust in God's promises and providence. This allowed him to reassure his frightened servant with confidence in God's protection and sovereignty.

In contrast, the servant's perspective was clouded by fear and doubt. His initial reaction was shaped by what he could physically see—the encircling enemy army—rather than trusting in God's unseen spiritual reality. Elisha's prayer for the servant's eyes to be opened was a call to shift his focus from the physical threat to God's greater spiritual truth.

Understanding these dynamics helps you appreciate the complexity of human perception. While physical sight is indispensable, acknowledging its limitations prompts you to seek spiritual insight and discernment. Recognizing God's presence and purposes beyond what your physical eyes can perceive enables you to navigate life with faith, courage, and wisdom. As you cultivate spiritual vision, you gain clarity, courage, and a deeper understanding of God's sovereign plan in your life.

Like Elisha's servant, my parents' lives were dictated by what the world wanted them to have. They empowered the world to place limits on their potential and growth. They had become comfortable. My sight caused me to break through the comfortability and break out of the box that I was placed in. I began to blossom.

Potential

For my potential to be realized, I had to stretch myself. Being enrolled in honor classes challenged me intellectually. The classes opened my mind to learning, not just being taught. Learning is when one has a thirst for understanding and becomes a sponge, searching for and soaking up knowledge. Education is vital to growth and development. When you stop learning, you stop growing. It is important to aspire to new levels. But to get to these new levels, there are steps one must take to progress. Below are the steps that I took.

Step one: I challenged myself by identifying at least three things I believed were beyond my capabilities but were needed for me to get to the next level. I challenged myself by taking honors courses, applying for colleges, and researching scholarships to help fund my education.

In my senior year, I was dedicated to finding a college to attend. As I reflect on this time, I see I was behind in this area. I should have started applying to colleges at the beginning of my junior year. I was doubtful that my dream to attend college was possible, and fearful of going off on a new adventure and leaving behind my family. I still did not fully believe college was possible for me. My parents could not afford to send me. The probability of my vision becoming a reality was low. However, I buckled down and pressed forward. Ms. Davis helped me pick out three schools: Penn State, Creighton University, and a college in California, the name of which I do not recall.

I received an acceptance letter from Creighton University in Omaha, Nebraska. I did not receive a response from the other two universities, and I was not willing to wait. I knew if I waited, I might back out, or something else might stop me from going. One must be active to gain traction.

I chose to keep moving. I secured two academic scholarships, totaling about three thousand dollars. The remainder of my education was financed with student loans and grants. I packed my bags.

Who would have thought that an African American urban girl would move to a small rural city to attend school? The school was located in downtown Omaha, and there was nothing around it. Today, it is highly populated and has all the amenities. But when I attended, it was a ghost town. There was nothing in the area within walking distance, which was a shock for me. I went from being able to walk or ride wherever I wanted to go to being isolated with no transportation. But even though I felt physically stuck, I knew this move was the biggest I had ever taken in getting un-stuck from my family's trajectory. You must change the perspective on your view of your environment in order to expand capabilities and tap into potential.

Step two: I created an inner circle to hold me accountable to leveling up. Mrs. Davis held me accountable. Ms. Davis and I met twice a week. I sought her advice as I reached milestones. I would meet with her after my classes or on my lunch break to get her advice on decisions I had to make. While others were eating lunch, I was focused on being mentored.

I sought her advice on running for Senior Class President.

She looked at me and said, "You should do it. What is stopping you?"

I thought, "*She's right. What is stopping me?*"

My response? Me.

I ran for Senior Class President and won. I was amazed—I did not think I would win. I did not run with the crowd. I was not an introvert; I was just not a conformer. I focused on forging my way. I had ditched the "Follow Me Syndrome" and instead focused on my books and the pursuit of my vision. I recall a conversation I had with a former classmate who was popular.

I asked her, "Why was I elected?"

She replied, "You're smart. You will lead us in the direction that we need to go."

I was humbled by her words and trust in me.

The other person in my circle was Ms. Georgia Harris, a vice president in a large pharmaceutical company. I met Georgia Harris in my freshman year of college. I worked at Sandoz Chemical for two summers, where Georgia served as a leader in the C-suite. Georgia became a mentor to me in those first two years. She was a leader that I aspired to emulate. Georgia taught me that every person mattered. She believed a leader should know every person in the company, regardless of their title, to reinforce that the individual is valuable. I was in awe of her character. She made every person feel special and appreciated.

The individuals I surrounded myself with forced me to action. I was with others who sparked my light. They ignited me to move. I was surrounded by individuals who were smarter than me. I learned that you must not be the smartest person in the room. If you are, you are placing a lid on growth and potential.

Because of my circle, I graduated from high school second in my class (Salutatorian) and was elected Senior Class President. I believed and had faith that I could go to college. My circle taught me to keep aiming higher. I did not stop with college. I continued my education and obtained an MBA. I kept my eye on the vision that they helped me to believe in. I saw that I did not have to settle. I could aspire for more. I had tapped into what was inside of me—potential—and used it to realize my vision.

I could leave behind the habits and beliefs of my childhood; I could go shopping more than twice in a year. I had been introduced to another way.

Step three: I was consistent. I took steps every week to keep moving forward.

I incorporated F.A.T., that is, Faith to Act and Think, into my mindset. My family did not have the means to pay for higher education; however, I had faith. I believed that the resources I needed would be provided, and they were. I received four scholarships, and the remainder of my college tuition was paid through grants and loans. I found a way. I did not give up on leveling up in my life. I did not let my potential remain dormant. As Margaret Atwood says, "Potential has a shelf life." [3] I was not going to miss out on opportunities and let my potential expire. I was determined to break the limits that had been set for my life.

I paved my way. I had determination, and I was going to go as far as I could. But there was one thing missing. I had to gain clarity toward my gift and apply it to my cause. I had to uncover what makes me uncomfortable and angry. I had to answer these questions: What would set me on fire? What could I do and not grow weary?

Answering these questions would require me to go deep within myself to gain an understanding of what I was to do with my life. What are your answers to these questions? Take time to pause and reflect before moving on to the next chapter.

---

3 Margaret Atwood, *Cat's Eye* (Vintage, 1998).

Chapter 3

THE PLAN

> *The only thing worse than being blind is having sight but no vision.*
>
> – HELEN KELLER

I returned to Chicago after I graduated from college. I found a decent job and rented my first apartment. Life was going well. I was happy and content.

I had achieved a major milestone; however, I needed to expand my vision so I could keep growing. You cannot stop once you reach the milestone. You owe it to yourself to keep going and realize even higher levels of achievement. If I didn't keep pushing myself, the happiness and contentment I felt would become obstacles toward finding even deeper joy and fulfillment. To achieve joy and fulfillment, I keep my commitment to growing and learning; after two years, I returned to graduate school.

It is important to have a plan. Jesus said to his disciples in John 14:4, "You know the way to the place where I am going." You are in control of you. Where you will go. How far you will go. The "where" and "how" are contingent upon your navigation. Navigation requires purpose, management, and skill. Purpose is the direction. You manage the obstacles and path for the journey. Skills utilize the potential and gift in you. Applying purpose, management, and skill enables you to make informed decisions and adjust to challenges throughout the journey of your life.

Along this journey, there will be numerous destinations. Destinations are not the end, but temporary stops. Temporary, because you are on a journey that does not cease until death. You aspire to travel to new locations, embracing new experiences and adventures. This form of traveling is similar to going on vacations. Vacations are visits to new destinations. Seeing new sights. Creating new experiences and memories. The desire is to keep going to new places. Remaining in one destination will cause you to become stagnant and complacent, hindering growth and evolution.

Challenge yourself by striving to reach new destinations. Progress to new levels in your life, and keep navigating your journey. To navigate requires self-awareness, decision making, adaptability, resilience, and a sense of purpose. Understand your values, set meaningful goals, and make the choices that align with your aspirations. Navigation is a continual process. The destination does not remain the same. Your journey is never-ending. Aspire to keep progressing, not giving up until the day you die. Self-discovery and growth are a continuous journey to navigate. Apply purpose, management, and skills to maximize the potential that will pave the way to new destinations.

It is easy to get swept away by the urgent tasks that demand our attention. The mind naturally focuses on safety and security, and we believe once we complete these urgent tasks, we will be secure. However, that is not always the case. Sometimes, what is urgent is not actually vital, and what is vital gets neglected because it does not seem urgent. You must take control of these instincts and determine for yourself what is urgent and what is vital.

Vital tasks are the most important things that must be done even though there may be no immediate consequences. For example, eating is not necessarily urgent. You can miss a meal without facing severe repercussions. However, eating is vital to survival. If you avoid eating for extended periods of time, you will inevitably see the long-term impact on your health.

Urgent tasks, on the other hand, are not vital to your survival. However, if you delay them, they do have immediate consequences. For example, you don't need to answer an email to survive. But if you don't answer it today, your employees will have problems tomorrow.

While both types of tasks are important, they can fall out of balance. Tasks that seem urgent can draw us away from the most vital things we need to do. And often, what we see as urgent is not so urgent after all.

Creating a plan ahead of time will help you differentiate between the two. Without a plan, you will drift. If you follow only what is urgent and neglect what is vital, you will arrive at an end point you never intended or desired.

It is crucial to remember the timeless wisdom in Luke 14:28–30: "Suppose one of you wants to build a tower. Won't you first sit down and estimate the cost to see if you have enough money to complete it? For if you lay the foundation and are not able to finish it, everyone who sees it will ridicule you, saying, 'This person began to build and wasn't able to finish.'" This powerful passage reminds us of the importance of planning, laying a solid foundation, and seeing our endeavors through to completion. Planning is not urgent, but it is vital. It is essential for achieving success in any endeavor.

There are two principles of planning. The first is that planning is the cornerstone of success. Just as a builder meticulously plans every aspect of a construction project before breaking ground, you too must carefully consider your goals, objectives, and strategies before embarking on any endeavor. Planning brings clarity to your vision, identifies potential obstacles, and charts a course of action towards your desired outcome.

The second principle is that laying a solid foundation is paramount for long-term success. Just as a building's foundation provides stability and support for the structure above, a strong foundation in your endeavors ensures resilience in the face of challenges and setbacks. This foundation may include cultivating essential skills, building strong relationships, or establishing sound systems to sustain your efforts over time.

COMPLETE THE EQUATION

Planning and laying a foundation are only half of the equation. The true test of success lies in your ability to finish what you start. As Luke 14:29 warns, failing to complete what you have begun can lead to ridicule and disappointment. Therefore, it is essential to maintain focus, perseverance, and determination to reach your goals.

It is important to plan, lay a solid foundation, and see your endeavors through to completion. Apply the principles in this scripture to your endeavors to build a future filled with success, fulfillment, and purpose. Plan diligently, lay a firm foundation, and finish strong, knowing that your efforts will not be in vain.

Conformity is often the easiest path. There are those who refuse to bend to the whims of societal pressures. They are the ones who stand tall, unwavering in their convictions, even in the face of adversity.

The story of Shadrach, Meshach, and Abednego from the book of Daniel serves as an example of the strength that comes from holding steadfast to one's beliefs. In Daniel 3:13–27, the three men refuse to bow down to a golden idol. King Nebuchadnezzar challenges their strength by threatening to cast them into a blazing furnace. The threat of the furnace does not deter them from standing their ground. The three men have unwavering faith to combat Nebuchadnezzar's arrogance and tyranny. Shadrach, Meshach, and Abednego choose to withstand the challenges of their environment rather than compromise their principles. Their actions teach a valuable lesson: true strength lies in standing firm, even when flames of opposition are raging. In the end, the three men do get thrown into the fire, but miraculously, they come out unscathed. Because of the three men's boldness, the King recognizes that they worship the only true God.

Even though these men were saved without harm, the consequences of Shadrach, Meshach, and Abednego's refusal were severe and real. They were facing death. They stood resolute, guided by their belief in someone greater than themselves. Their story reminds us that sometimes, you must be willing to face the fire to uphold your beliefs.

Standing for what you believe in is not always easy. It requires courage, determination, and willingness to endure hardship. But the rewards are immeasurable. Standing firm in the face of adversity cultivates resilience, strengthens character, and produces personal growth.

Resilience is born out of struggle. It is forged in the flames of adversity, refined by the challenges faced. By choosing to withstand the trials of life rather than succumb to them, you emerge stronger and more resilient than before.

Trials also shape your character. They test your integrity and force you to confront your values head-on. In doing so, you develop a deeper understanding of yourself and what you stand for. Your convictions become a guiding force, shaping the decisions you make and the paths you choose to follow.

Ultimately, the outcome of standing firm is growth. Through adversity, you discover your true strength and potential. You learn valuable lessons that shape you into a better, more compassionate individual. Like Shadrach, Meshach, and Abednego, you emerge from the fire transformed, ready to face whatever challenges lie ahead.

In a world that often seeks to tear you down, take inspiration from Shadrach, Meshach, and Abednego. Stand strong, unwavering in your beliefs, and embrace the flames of adversity as opportunities for growth and transformation. For it is through standing firm that you discover the true depth of your strength and the power of your convictions.

Like Shadrach, Meshach, and Abednego, I would not back down from the pursuit of my plan. My plan was to live the best life that I could—being whole and complete, leaving no potential unused. I wanted no excuses and no procrastination. Going forward was the only option. I had determination, and I was committed.

I attended school part-time while working part-time. I landed a job at a corporation that was hiring a bookkeeper. I worked three days a week, eight hours a day. I attended school on the days that I did not work. This was the perfect schedule to support my vision.

When you are following the path that is for you, resources that you need will be provided to make your vision a reality. Positive thinking will also aid in providing the resources you need. If you believe in what you are doing, a way will be made and what is needed will be provided. One must believe and have faith. I was attending graduate school, working a part-time job, had a car, and I was able to afford a one-bedroom apartment in a decent neighborhood.

Do not be swayed from your vision just because the resources you need are not immediately available. Holding off because of a lack of resources means you do not have faith in what you are striving to achieve. Failing to move forward means that you have no hope.

Instead, let hope be your foundation. My hope caused me to jump out of bed each day. I was motivated and inspired to act. I had a vision of becoming a female executive at a major corporation, being a vital team player in supporting the mission. This vision drove me to keep going. I knew I could be an asset. I just needed to land at a company where my talents would be utilized.

Once I obtained my master's degree, I landed a job that paid a decent salary at an aviation consulting company. We developed financial and engineering plans for airport development programs. However, something was not right. I was not fulfilled. I was still thirsty. I kept drinking the water, but the water was not satisfying my thirst. I was merely drifting along in my career. There was something missing. I did not yet know what the something was.

The company was lacking. It was a good company, but management placed limits on the team members. My vision was partially being realized. I was an executive sitting at the table, but I did not fit in. I was restless with management and the constraints of the company. I am not a conformer, so I bumped heads with senior leadership. I was viewed as difficult because I spoke my mind. I was not insubordinate; I just did not believe in going along with the crowd when it was in opposition to my values or when I was being devalued.

One night at dinner with a group of peers and senior management, I was giving my input on the company's lack of inclusion and diversity. I was the only female at dinner, surrounded by white males. The men on my job were perpetuating the stereotypes of gender roles in the workplace. It angered me that the men viewed women as inferior. Their view was that women were to be silent, manipulated, and denied a voice.

In the company, females primarily held positions in administrative support functions while the males held positions as consultants and in senior management. At this dinner, I brought up an idea to break the barriers by launching an initiative to partner with minority organizations. This would not only be good for the minority organizations; it would also improve the image of firm, which people believed was lacking in equity and inclusion. The company had no women or men of color in leadership roles.

The supervisor replied, "Well, maybe this is a good suggestion, but maybe it should not be you."

I countered, "Why not me?"

He blustered back, saying, "You are young and lack experience on making connections." What he really meant was that I was a woman. No woman in the company had taken the initiative to break the glass ceiling. I was the first female consultant in the company.

I countered again, "Age does not dictate a person's capabilities. Do not judge a book by its cover."

I struck out to prove him wrong. God is clear on His creation, creating both male and female in His image. He gave every person the authority to be imitators of Christ. We are one humanity, distinct by our gender, but with every person having a role to play in this world. Men and women can both work and be included in leadership roles. Men must stop seeing women in cultural terms and instead see women as God does. Perspectives on gender can change with love. This means encouraging and promoting women to see their value as God sees their value.

I was not going to allow the environment of the company to place limits on my capabilities. I wanted to learn. I made connections and aided the company in securing two major contracts.

If you choose to allow others to control who you are and what you can do, you will not search within yourself to find who you are. Making connections and communicating with individuals became one of my strengths. I enjoyed meeting with individuals, learning about them and what they thought, what they did, and why they chose what they did. If I had allowed senior management to place me in a box, I would have remained in a box.

In the movie *The Woman King*, a woman and general named Nanisca commanded an all-female army to protect the West African kingdom of Dahomey. The kingdom of Dahomey was a major source of slaves in the slave trade. Nanisca sought to put an end to her people being taken as slaves. She chose to fight. Fighting is what one must do to realize one's vision. One cannot allow others to place limits on what is achievable. Nanisca was victorious in saving her people. She was crowned the Woman King.

King Ghezo, at Nanisca's inauguration ceremony, made a powerful statement that rings true to me. For people to be enslaved, they must first believe they are slaves. The mind is power. What you believe is what will be. One must take control of their mind and not allow others to have control.

This is what I had to do at this job. I was not going to allow others to dictate what I believed about me. I was driven. I had a thirst to become better. I believed in myself even if the males in the company did not. My tenure with this company was about five years. I moved on after seeing that the barriers in the company could not be torn down. The beliefs and values were too entrenched. They would stifle my growth and development, and I was not going to settle for a place that would control who I could become.

I knew that there was more for me. The restlessness in me was calling me to leave. The Spirit was leading me away. It said, "It is time to move on." I was obedient and followed.

It is imperative to move when you are told to move. Failing to move will result in missed opportunities and growth; opportunities that may not be presented again; opportunities that lead to growth because you are challenged and stretched. I continued to move on to different companies, holding leadership positions.

Ultimately, I landed a job with a government agency.

I thought, "Wow, now I can make a difference."

Again, I ran into barriers and roadblocks that attempted to dictate my mindset and beliefs. I determined that working for someone else was not in my best interest. I had to develop a plan.

The Spirit was calling me to become an entrepreneur. I became energized. I was on fire. I was researching businesses online and came across an opportunity to be a franchise owner with Edible Arrangements. I had a close friend who was interested in collaborating with me, so we partnered together on this venture. I was so excited. I was going to own my business. I hired my sister to be the store manager. She was also excited aboutabout this new opportunity.

I just knew this was the business for me. It was a business that aligned with my values. I could serve others by providing them with a healthy product to complement their special occasions. I was all in. I was elated.

All About Me

This business was all about me and what I wanted. I came to learn this was my downfall. Joyce Meyer states that we must give up our right to put ourselves first to find true joy and a closer relationship with God.[4] I realized that being all about me was a hindrance to true wellness and joy.

John 15:5 states "Apart from me you can do nothing." I sputtered along in the business for four years due to a lost connection to God. I was the focal point instead of God. I had to get out of the way. However, I had to suffer through the process before learning how to die to myself and live for God. I needed to see with His eyes and not my eyes, living in alignment with the Spirit.

I kept pressing forward with full steam. I believed that at the five-year mark, I would turn the corner from surviving to thriving. I ran through my savings and accumulated debt. I was listening to others who kept cheering me on, telling me to keep going and that it often takes five years for a business to become viable.

This advice proved to be wrong. I was not going to make this business work because it was not the business for me. I had missed a

---

[4] Joyce Meyer, *What About Me?: Get Out of Your Own Way and Discover the Power of an Unselfish Life* (FaithWords, 2024).

major step: getting in alignment with the Spirit to see if this was the path to take. I looked at this business using only my sight. I failed to reflect, meditate, and talk with the Spirit. I was busy looking with my eyes and picked the first business opportunity that came along.

I chose to keep going, ignoring the countless signs that screamed, "STOP." I encountered issues that should have given me pause. Know that it is never too late to turn back. You do not have to keep going.

My partner and I had a difficult time finding a location. The location we wanted was not accepted by the franchise. Ironically, after we opened our franchise about two years later, the company approached us to set up a store in the area we initially wanted. Next was the cost to build out the franchise. The costs were about forty percent higher than what the company originally estimated. Last was the corporate environment. The corporation was about making money. All supplies had to be purchased through the company, even though the items could be procured at a lesser expense elsewhere. They required that we participate in co-op advertisements, even though the advertisements did not provide a return on what I had expended. The marketing media selected for our area did not match the market. The company did not consider the characteristics of each market and allow the owner to determine the best course of action for advertising. I was throwing away money toward a marketing program that yielded no return.

At each obstacle, the Spirit would say, "You must get out of this business. Cut your losses and stop." However, I kept moving ahead with the franchise.

My continuous restlessness should have been another major sign. I thought the franchise would be the solution to my restlessness. Instead, the store became felt like my prison. I did like working with the customers. However, I felt contained because I had to be in the store at specific times and days of the week. Being confined is not a business for me. I must be free to move about and have flexibility to go in another direction.

I began to dread going into the store. I saw the store as an anchor around my neck. I distanced myself from staff. I continued to handle the day-to-day operations from home. I did not go into the store more than one day a week. My partner and I began actively looking for a buyer and found one. A solution was provided for the problem I created. After four years in this franchise, I had drained my savings and amassed twenty-five thousand dollars in debt.

This business cost me more than just time and money. It cost me my relationship with my sister. My sister was the store manager. She joined me in this venture. She believed in my vision. She worked alongside me, hoping to make the business work. If it were not for her, the business would have been sold much earlier. She worked tirelessly, six days a week—sometimes seven if there was a holiday. She was committed to making the business viable. I greatly appreciated her enthusiasm and energy. Part of the reason I stayed in the business longer than I should have was that I wanted to make it work for her sake. I used my income, my savings, and credit cards to pay her and the staff.

I should have seen that I was asking too much of her. She was carrying the burden of the business. Instead, I was focused on seeing only what I wanted to see, missing the impact the business was having on her. It was all about me and what I wanted. I was disappointed in the business, so I lost sight of her needs and the needs of my employees. My disappointment was fueled by selfishness and caused me to be disconnected. I was focused on self-gratification instead of serving and responding to the needs of those around me. This was another sign that I was not moving in alignment the Spirit: my selfishness was allowing the business to run my sister into the ground.

Ultimately, my sister stopped talking to me. One day, she just stopped showing up to work. I did not know she had stopped showing up until there was an issue at the store. One of the employees contacted me because no one was available to assist. It was then, in the fourth year, that I realized both my sister and my business partner had abandoned ship. I was so busy looking at only me that I failed to see the impact the business was having on the two of them.

Philippians 2:3–4 states, "Do nothing out of selfish ambition or vain conceit. Rather, in humility value others above yourself, not looking to your own interests but each of you to the interest of the others." I was out for my own interest and lacked humility. I was not applying what I had learned from my mentors, Georgia and Ms. Davis. I had missed the mark. I needed a dose of harsh reality to show me that the world did not revolve around me and that what others need is paramount.

Give people what they want, and you will get what you want. I had to first give a hand before asking for a hand.

Ask Him

Reflecting on this time, I believe the Spirit did tell me that I was to be an entrepreneur, just not an owner of an Edible Arrangements franchise. I was not listening, not paying attention. The decision to own a franchise was based on what I chose to see. This franchise resulted in an invaluable lesson: lean not on your own understanding but question the basis of your understanding. What makes you think this is the way to go? Identify the indicators pointing you in this direction. You must question the basis of your decisions.

This business was not going to work from the onset. Besides the many other flashing indicator lights, the biggest was that I did not look to God, the One who makes all possible. As Job 12:10 states, "In his hand is the life of every creature and the breath of all mankind." He makes plans a reality and brings forth the resources needed.

I did not consult with him before making my decision to invest in the franchise. The decision was based on my selfishness. In trying to satisfy my restlessness, I failed to see that my life was not about myself but about serving the Lord.

I neglected to ask Him, "What is it that you want me to do for you? Is this business what you would have me do?"

If I had asked these questions, he would have told me, "No."

Purpose is found by asking to join God in the work he is doing, not telling him to join me in the work I am doing. I had it backwards. My life is not my own.

When Jesus was praying in Gethsemane prior to his betrayal by Judas and his crucifixion, he said, "My Father, if it is possible, may this cup be taken from me. Yet not as I will, but as you will" (Matthew 26:39).

Jesus was in despair over what was to come. He left the place where he was praying to return to the disciples, who were sleeping. He did not stay with them. He had a burning desire to speak to his father.

He went away a second time to pray, "My Father, if it is not possible for this cup to be taken away unless I drink it, may your will be done" (Matthew 26:42).

Jesus was in anguish. He contemplated the pain sin would cause him to endure, the pain he would have to bear to save humanity. His purpose was to save mankind. To fulfill his purpose, he had to submit to the Father. He had to die and then rise again. To submit would result in anguish and pain that you and I cannot incomprehend.

This is what I had to understand and learn. I suffered in this business for four years to learn this lesson: that my life is not my own; it is God's. Just as Jesus was born to serve a purpose, so am I. I was created to serve his purpose. I had to learn that owning an Edible Arrangements franchise was not God's will for me. It was my will.

When you submit to the Father, he will show you the way. You will see what he sees for you. Seeing what he sees does not mean that you will not encounter hardship and suffering. You will endure pain, but you will be equipped to withstand it. You can withstand it because you have God. You are following his will, so you will be filled with peace during the storm and trials.

No person says, "I want to be in pain. I love pain. I seek to suffer." Instead, you say, "I want to follow his will because I believe. I have faith and hope. I am equipped and enabled to endure because I am doing the work of the Father." Know that he will take care of you. You are not alone. You have his presence and love. You will get through and receive the reward he has planned for you.

In Jeremiah 29:11–14, God says:

"For I know the plans I have for you, plans to prosper you and not to harm you, plans to give you hope and a future. Then you will call on me and come and pray to me, and I will listen to you. You will seek me and find me when you seek me with all your heart. I will be found by you and will bring you back from captivity. I will gather you from all the nations and places where I have banished you and will bring you back to the place from which I carried you into exile."

God's word is true. He does not break his promises. As such, I have faith and belief when I follow him. Doing the work he has instructed me to do makes me want to move forward in fulfilling the purpose of my creation. At times, the road traveled will appear to be unbearable. However, leaning into the Spirit will equip you to get through. Instead of looking at the road with physical sight, use your spiritual sight to look to the future—the future God has promised you, the future you will realize and achieve when following Him. Do his will and not yours.

After selling the franchise, my vision of being an entrepreneur was not dampened. I had fallen but not failed. There is a difference between "falling" and "failing." Failing and falling are two distinct concepts. Both can be temporary setbacks; however, both can lead to success. Both can result in transformation and learning.

Falling is a physical descent from a higher to a lower position. It can be accidental or intentional. In the pursuit of success, falling can represent stumbling or experiencing setbacks along the way. These can be moments of weakness, mistakes, or unexpected challenges that temporarily slow down progress. We must acknowledge the reality that setbacks are a natural part of any journey towards success. Falling can sometimes lead to failing, especially if it results in a failure to accomplish something due to the fall itself. But falling does not necessarily result in failure. The setbacks are a vehicle for learning. We must get back up and continue to press forward. Bouncing forward is resiliency.

Failing, on the other hand, means not meeting an intended goal or expectation. It is often associated with shortcomings or inadequacies in achieving a desired outcome. Failure is not permanent unless one misses the opportunity to learn. One must analyze why the failure occurred, adjust strategies, and persevere. Failure can be a result of various factors, such as a lack of effort, insufficient skills or resources, or external circumstances. However, individuals can often overcome initial setbacks and continue progressing towards their goals.

Both falling and failing can be temporary in the pursuit of success. Both experiences can provide valuable lessons and opportunities for growth, ultimately contributing to future success. The point is to get back up when you fall, "for though the righteous fall seven times, they rise again" (Proverbs 24:16). You must bounce forward when you fail, for "if you falter in a time of trouble, how small is your strength!" (Proverbs 24:10).

I got back up. This setback was not going to stop me from achieving that which I wanted and believed in. I was going to take this experience and apply it to my next business. I had to be patient about what I was to own. In due time, I would know.

What I did know was that I had to let my next steps be led by God. I had a vision that would be realized. I had to spend time in the desert being equipped to handle the vision. There was a plan for my life.

There is much work to do in this world—work that adds value to our communities and others. Deep inside, we know this. M. Scott Peck puts it well: "Each of us is born for a purpose, and we want our lives to matter. I don't think it's unique to only some of us; it's a longing of every human being."[5] One must identify their gifts so they can be used make a difference. I had to uncover my work.

---

5   M. Scott Peck, *The Road Less Traveled: A New Psychology of Love, Traditional Values and Spiritual Growth* (Simon & Schuster, 1978).

Chapter 4
THE WAY TO THE PLAN

It is on the strength of observation and reflection that one finds a way. So, we must dig and delve unceasingly.

– CLAUDE MONET

The journey to realizing your vision often starts with a small seed of an idea or dream. That small seed is what you must pay attention. It is the miniscule that provides focus and direction and sprouts into something big. At first, it may seem insignificant, almost imperceptible amid the vastness of the world around you. With consistent effort and dedication, that small seed has the potential to grow into something significant and impactful.

Just like the parable of the growing seed in Mark 4, in which a man scattered his seed and day after day witnessed its growth, your vision requires consistent and purposeful daily actions. Each action you take contributes to the nurturing of that seed, gradually bringing it closer to fruition. Even when progress seems slow or obstacles arise, continuing to sow the seeds of your vision ensures that you are on the path towards your desired outcome.

The seed described in Mark 4:28 grows through a process: "First the stalk, then the head, then the full kernel in the head." It took time for the seed to produce. Day after day, it continued to grow through persistent dedication and belief. Similarly, your vision undergoes a process of development. There are phases of growth and maturation. Each stage builds upon the previous stage until finally, reaching the full realization of our vision.

It's crucial to recognize and celebrate the signs of progress along the way. These signs serve as reminders that your efforts are not in vain and that your vision is indeed taking shape.

Ultimately, like the farmer who patiently awaited the harvest, you must trust in the process. Have faith that your consistent actions will yield the results you seek. As you persistently sow the seeds of your vision, you pave the way for its eventual manifestation, just as the soil produces the grain in due time.

There is a plan for you. God gives you the strength and power to press forward. His plans cannot be overcome and will not fail. This is a promise for you to believe, holding onto faith that the invisible will become visible. Your consistent actions that will produce the type of vision that withstands the test of time.

In Mark 6, Jesus returns to his hometown of Nazareth to teach in the synagogue. However, instead of being met with faith and acceptance, he encounters skepticism and doubt from those who knew him. Despite witnessing his miracles and hearing his teachings, the people of Nazareth fail to believe in him. In Mark 6:6, the text says that Jesus "was amazed at their lack of faith." These words encapsulate a profound truth about the human condition: we have a vast capacity for unbelief and contempt, which hinders us from realizing the full extent of what can be achieved.

The lack of faith Jesus sees highlights the profound impact unbelief can have on a person's life. Unbelief is a pervasive barrier that prevents us from embracing the possibilities that lie beyond our immediate comprehension. It restricts vision, confines potential, and blinds us to the extraordinary opportunities awaiting. Allowing doubt to cloud judgment limits and stifles the growth that comes from embracing the unknown.

The contempt that the people of Nazareth had for Jesus exacerbated the problem of their unbelief. If we dismiss something or someone out of disdain or a sense of superiority, we close ourselves off to understanding and empathy. Contempt breeds arrogance and closes the door to meaningful connections and transformative experiences. Instead of learning from others or appreciating different perspectives, we remain entrenched in our narrow-mindedness, unable to see the beauty and richness of diversity.

The story in Mark 6 serves as a powerful reminder to cultivate faith and humility in your life. Faith enables you to transcend limitations and tap into the boundless potential that lies within you. It empowers you to embrace uncertainty with courage and approach life with openness and receptivity.

Similarly, humility fosters a sense of reverence and awe for the world around you. It is a reminder of your inherent fallibility and the need to remain open in the face of the unknown. By acknowledging limitations and embracing a posture of humility, you create space for growth and discovery. The people of Nazareth missed the opportunity for growth and discovery due to their unbelief and contempt.

I would have to cling to humility and belief for what I had to go through next.

Get Through the Desert

God rescued the Israelites who had been in bondage for over four hundred years. Moses was appointed to lead them out of Egypt. God chose the longest route to the promised land.

Though they didn't realize it, the longest route was what they needed to prepare for what was to come. The Israelites required preparation. They needed to build their strength and stamina. Bondage had trained and programmed their minds to be negative and think of themselves as inferior. Each time they encountered a struggle or battle, they immediately desired to turn back and give up on having more. They were eager to give up because they had been oppressed for so long that submission had become part of their DNA. Their oppression caused them to have low self-esteem and a lack of confidence. All their lives, they had been devalued and mistreated. They had come to accept this as their way of life. Their environment dictated what they could see and placed a cap on their aspirations.

They lacked spiritual sight.

It was inconceivable to the Israelites that they could obtain a land that was abundant in resources, be free to do what they wanted, and not have to answer to a tyrant. Because of their lack of belief and sight, they needed to spend time in the desert, which was their training ground. Many did not make it due to their obstinance.

Just like the Israelites, I spent time in a desert where I encountered obstacles to aid me in growing. I faced situations that equipped and empowered me to become who I am today. I required training and preparation. We often think of the desert as a desolate or forbidding area. It is seen as a wilderness— place where there is scarcity of resources. There may be sandstorms. Travelers will be thirsty and hungry, trying to search for sustenance.

While all these may be true, a season in the desert also aids you in developing perseverance and tenacity to keep pressing forward, particularly when you know that you will get to a land that is plentiful. I had to go through a desert to expand in abundance, success, and love. My desert opened my eyes to see beyond surviving.

NOT SURVIVE BUT THRIVE

When my mother became ill, my father became her caretaker. I wanted to believe that all was well. I did not want to see that there was a problem. I sought to avoid the situation, looking the other way so I would not have to see her deterioration. But the reality was that my mom was becoming childlike. She could not walk or speak. Her eyes were vacant. She looked at me but did not *see* me.

One day, I received a call from my sister that made me finally face the reality that life must change. She stated that Mom was not doing well at home. She had been admitted to the hospital, only to have my father take her out against the doctor's orders. We needed to step in. The parents I knew had aged. Age had impacted their health and ability to take care of themselves. Moreover, my mom was diabetic, and her diabetes was getting progressively worse. She was on insulin three times a day. The diabetes was causing further complications in her health. My parents needed the help of their children to survive.

My siblings and I needed to get my mother the help and care she needed. I met my brother at my parents' house. My mom was in bad shape—in bed, incoherent. She could not speak, walk, or move. Her bed and clothes were soiled. It was a picture that no child would want to see of their mom. I broke down crying, devastated at what I saw.

Immediately, we knew my mom had to be removed from the home. She required medical care that my father was not capable of providing. I believed she may have suffered a stroke; however, my parents were close-mouthed. They were not forthcoming in what was going on with them medically, financially, or personally. They did not believe in sharing any information about their finances or health with their children. I will never know why. However, this was their way and practice.

My brother and I cleaned Mom up and carried her out of the house. My father sat in his favorite chair in the living room. He attempted to stop us, but my brother stepped in. The situation could have gotten ugly; however, I believe my father knew it was best for my mother to leave. He watched us leave, and I saw the pain in his face. He could see that the life he had grown accustomed to was over. My mother was not in any shape to remain in the home. He was devastated.

My brother and I temporarily moved my mom to her sister's house until we were able to place her into a rehabilitation facility. We had hoped she would recover in the rehabilitation center; however, she did not quickly recover. Her medical condition was unstable for about six months. Ultimately, she was diagnosed with dementia and congestive heart failure. The doctor's prognosis was that she would not recover. The doctors had no way of determining how long she would live. The best her family could do was make her remaining days comfortable.

As my mom's deterioration progressed in the nursing facility, I discovered that my father was diagnosed with Alzheimer's. I am not sure when he was first diagnosed because he never shared this diagnosis with his children. This would explain his irrational decision to remove my mother from the hospital and his hostile behavior towards my brother and sister. I know his secretiveness was a result of selfishness on his part, but not in a mean way. He just did not want us to know. He did not want to give up his independence. He clung to the life he had grown accustomed to, living in the home he had built for his family and wife.

It soon became clear that my dad could not remain in the house alone. He started wandering the streets. A neighbor informed my brother that he saw my dad walking around lost. The three of us agreed to place my father in a nursing and rehabilitation center. He was placed in a center that was secure because he was a wanderer, which is one symptoms of the disease. As soon as a door was opened, he would escape.

The first home was too expensive, so he had to be moved to another facility. But at the second facility, my father got into an altercation with another resident who called him a "nigger." Fighting was not tolerated at the facility, which is understandable. However, what was not acceptable was that the other resident received no repercussions for *his* behavior.

My father was now at his third facility. This was a man who was accustomed to coming and going as he wanted. He had been placed in three different, unfamiliar environments in less than six months. He was confused and depressed. I visited him at least once a week.

I would also take him to visit my mom.

His last visit with my mom broke my heart. They were sitting in her room, just holding hands. My mom could not talk. She just looking at him.

My dad said to her, "Momma." This was his nickname for her. "You are here because I cannot take care of you. I believe this is the best place for you. I miss and love you."

My mother just looked; she could not speak.

We left the facility, and I took my father back to his nursing facility that was about twenty miles away. Because of my parents' conditions, they required different types of care. This meant they could not be in the same location. I am sure this broke my father's heart even more.

I will never know what he thought of himself during this time. I can only imagine that he thought he had failed his wife. He was not able to provide for her as he had been all his life. I know in his moments of clarity, he was depressed over how his life had evolved. He had gone from living in his home to being contained in a facility apart from his wife. His living conditions impacted his thinking, causing further decline in his health. He gave up on life.

One hot summer day about two months later, I was standing in line at a restaurant when my phone rang.

The voice said, "You need to go to St. James Hospital now. We found your father not breathing in his room. He was unresponsive."

I rushed to the hospital, calling my siblings on the way. My brother met me there. My sister was unable to meet us. My brother and I were taken to a small private room. A doctor came in to meet with us. The doctor informed us that my dad had passed.

My father's death released a tightly wound spring and caused my family to spiral out of control. My family had lost the head of our household.

As I tried to make sense of this change, I visited my mom in the healthcare facility three times a week. You must be present and visible in facilities, or your loved one could be mistreated. I saw the way others were treated who had no visitors. My mom did not talk. Dementia had taken over. She lived in her private world. She did not speak and made no attempts to communicate. She was slowly passing away before my eyes. The entire time I would visit, we just sat together. I wanted her to know she was not alone.

Watching what occurred with my mom and dad made me realize that life is to be lived. To live, I had to take control of my health. My mom and dad were both homebodies. They did not venture out much or do any physical activity. The most activity they did in a day was go to the grocery store. Every now and then, they'd go visit a friend, but this was rare. Their life lacked activity, purpose, and drive. They were not motivated to get involved in community events, find a hobby, or join organizations to learn. Their minds were closed to learning more. They had settled for what life had given them instead of making a life.

Watching them, especially in this state, made me realize I must do better. I could not settle. I wanted to thrive—not just do enough to get by, but make a difference.

Finding Purpose

When a memory is so powerful it is never forgotten, psychologists call it a "core memory." It is not only something you'd never forget even if you lived to be a hundred and twenty years old, but it is also something that shapes you from that moment on. Its impact can cause your life to shift. You do not see it coming. It sneaks up on you, for better or worse, and pounces.

My father's death was a core memory for each of my siblings, and it changed each of us in different ways. His death certainly caused something to change in my brother. My brother spiraled out of control. I saw a change in him physically. He put on weight, took less care of his appearance, and lacked a zest for life. His marriage was rocky, and his finances were shaky. I could see that he was troubled and lost. He was drifting in life. He lacked focus on what he could do. He worked a job, but the job did not challenge him mentally. The job paid the bills and allowed him to maintain his household.

My brother had a gift in technology that he failed to see and cultivate. He allowed life to overwhelm him instead of choosing to take control. This left him open to negativity. You either control life, or life controls you. Life controls you when you are striving for the acceptance and pleasures of others—sacrificing yourself to please others instead of taking responsibility for yourself. Taking responsibility for yourself means consciously seeking to meet your needs and stay balanced, believing in the person you are. This responsibility allows you to face the discomfort, challenges, and adversities of life. My brother allowed life to control him.

I remember my brother and I were laughing and joking during the 2009 Valentine's Day weekend. He assisted me in making deliveries for my Edible Arrangements franchise. It was a long, hard weekend, and without him, I would not have been able to make all the deliveries. He was worn out from making the deliveries and dealing with customers. I treated him to dinner that weekend to show my appreciation. We went our separate ways from the restaurant.

His parting words to me were, "Don't call me, I'll call you."

I woke up the morning of February 18, 2009, feeling ill. I felt as if I should not go to work. I shook it off and went about my day. Later, I left work and went to the gym, as part of my normal routine. I always left my phone in the locker because this was my quiet time to relax, decompress, and regroup. I didn't want any distractions.

I completed my workout and returned to my locker to change my clothes. When I looked at my phone, I saw I had twenty missed calls. The majority were from my sister, plus a few calls from two friends. I immediately called my sister, who sounded hesitant to speak to me over the phone. All she said was that we needed to go to my brother's house; he needed our help.

She met me at my house, and we went to my brother's house. Along the way is when she told me the truth. My brother had been found dead in his home along with his wife. The police reported their deaths as a murder and suicide. My brother had shot his wife and then killed himself. His children were not harmed. I was devastated. This was a day I will never forget.

This was the second death in my family, following my father. My mom was sheltered in her cocoon, totally unaware of the state of her family.

My brother's wife's family took their grief out on me and my sister, not allowing us to see our nephews. I have not seen my nephews since February 2009. I think of them often, praying that they are doing well and that one day we will meet again.

My brother had his faults, but who doesn't? His way of thinking was a product of my mom and dad. My mother sheltered him from life's problems and blinded him to the real world. My mom's smothering caused him to be unable to face adversity. She lavished all her attention on my brother. He was the sun and the moon in her life. I believe this was because he was her only son. She had two daughters but only one son. My brother and father did not have a good relationship. My father was hostile towards my brother, jealous of their relationship and how my mother was unfairly biased towards her son.

My mother and brother's relationship was similar to that of Joseph and Jacob in the bible; Joseph was the favored sibling, which caused jealousy and dissension in the marriage and family. The jealousy of his siblings caused Joseph deep hardship, but it also launched Joseph onto his path to develop character for his assignments ahead. Ultimately, what happened to Joseph was in accordance with God's plan. But the similarities between Joseph and my brother end at the favoritism.

My brother did not see or appreciate the lessons presented to him during his time in this world. He was not able to withstand storms and trials on his own. Whenever he took a wrong turn or made a bad decision, my mom would come to his rescue. Whenever things were tight, he ran to her to bail him out. She was his security blanket. My mother's ever-present safety nets resulted in his fear of falling. Being sheltered, he lacked resilience. Falling to him meant failing because he did not know how to get back up on his own.

He did not understand the concept of sacrificing to grow. Growth requires seeing with the Spirit to have faith and hope that all will work out for good. God's word is clear: all is in accordance with his will and purpose for your good. This means you must surrender to his will and not be anxious or worried for an outcome because the outcome is in accordance with his way.

My brother never learned to rely on God. He relied on people. Surrendering to people is the greatest inhibitor toward seeing with the

Spirit. People are not to control our thinking; they are to support us as we develop behaviors that empower us to living a complete life.

My brother had to have his own way, but he was also loving, compassionate, and reliable. No friend of his would be in need. What was his, he would share. My parents instilled in their children that we must help our fellow brothers and sisters who are in need. If you have, then the other person has as well. There is no such thing as "mine only." It is ours. He just had no comprehension of hard work, following the journey to live a life of meaning and impact. God provides what we need. Our duty is to use what he gives us to obtain what we want.

Like Samson, the last judge in ancient Israel, my brother's choices in life ultimately caused his downfall. God blessed Samson with supernatural strength—strength that was to be used to help his people. Samson used his strength haphazardly, not appreciating the gift. He took it for granted. His downfall was the women he chose to associate with—in particular, the infamous Delilah. She was the kin of his enemy. She conspired with the Philistines to find the source of his strength so she could destroy him.

The same analogy applied to my brother. His downfall was the women he chose in his life—starting long before the woman he married. He was weak when it came to women. Although the women were not his enemies, they were not the type of women who would help him become his best self. My brother chose women that did not challenge him to grow and evolve; instead they enabled him to remain stagnant. They did not sharpen him to expand his mind to see beyond his physical sight. His life was based on assets instead of what he could create using his potential.

My brother's story had other similarities to Samson's as well.

Samson was a powerful man with supernatural strength. Likewise, my brother was a body builder, and his mind was strong, too. He built desktop computers from scratch. He had a knack for information and technology. My brother was a comedian, the life of the party. He would keep you in stitches. He had great strength and a loving heart.

Samson's death was a tragedy like was my brother's. In his final years, Samson was a slave for the Philistines, blindly grinding their grain and suffering from regret. He saw he had failed to complete the purpose for his life. His hair had grown back, and he sought to use his strength one final time. He called on God, pleading, "Sovereign Lord, remember me. Please, God, strengthen me just once more"(Judges 16:28).

Samson was physically blind, but his spiritual eyes were opened in this moment just before his death. Upon his death, Sampson killed more Philistines than he had in his lifetime. Samson spent his life chasing his own desires instead of placing God's purpose first and foremost. It took the loss of his eyesight for him to gain spiritual sight. I will always wonder if my brother found his sight before his death. I may have received a hint.

About six months after his death, I attended a conference for work where I met a gentleman who claimed he was a medium. He was able to speak to those "on the other side." I While God is opposed to believers seeking out mediums and psychics, he uses all things we do, even our sins, to awaken us to his truth. This is not a practice I advise, but at the time, I was looking for answers as to why I was still grieving and lost. God can and does use non-believers to reach us. He is in control no matter what. I believe God spoke through that man on this day to talk to me. I don't believe this man truly spoke with my brother, but I do believe God used my pain and what this man had to say to open my eyes.

The gentlemen stated that my brother said he was okay. He was no longer in pain and unhappy. "All his life," this man explained, "your brother pointed fingers at others when he should have been paying attention to the finger that was pointing back at him. He is finally at peace."

This was the message sent through him to me. I do not believe this message was from my brother. I believe God used it to open my mind to reflect on where I had come from, to where I am now, and where I needed to go.

In my reflections, I saw that there were once three musketeers: my brother, sister, and me, and now there were two. My brother's death left me heartbroken. My best friend was gone.

I was thinking, "What am I going to do? Why did he do this? Nothing in this life is so severe that it cannot be overcome."

I reflected on how my world had spiraled out of control. At times, I did not want to continue with my life. I thought of ways I could end my life. I expressed my thoughts to my friend, Nina. She immediately stated to me, "I do not want to hear you say this again. I rebuke these words in the name of Jesus."

I did not speak these words again; however, I continued to be miserable. All I kept thinking about was why it happened. What could I have done differently? How could I have stopped him?

I hit the darkest point in my life when my brother died. I took a detour on the journey to my purpose. I was at my most vulnerable. It took me ten years to accept that my brother's death was not a reflection of me. I spent a lot of time reflecting and reading God's word, talking to God, and looking to see with the Spirit. The Spirit provided me with the answers to my questions.

My brother's death was outside of my control. I could not have stopped him or kept him here. God had written the book for his life. His book was not to be a long novel but a short story. I was blessed to have had my brother in my life for the time that he was present. I appreciate and love the memories.

The Spirit had a future place for me; it required my full attention to reach the next destination in the journey of my life. I could finally see that my brother's death was the catalyst moving me forward to the next phase of my journey. I firmly belief that nothing happens that God does not allow. What he allows is part of his predestined plan for every person.

I am to use what happened to me to help others. I am to share my story to help others see not only what they want to see, but to look within themselves—to see their value and talent and use that talent to build a better life. I wanted to show people they need not be concerned with materialistic things, which come and go. They will fade with time. What does not fade is what is within. What is within gets better as time passes.

I want you to take time to think about where you have been, where you are now, and the picture you see of you in the future. Identify the growth, obstacles, and development that have gotten you where you are. In each period, there are lessons. Lessons to aid you in realizing the vision shared with you by the Spirit. It is our responsibility to live out our purpose achieve the vision for our life.

With grief and pain, one can learn. Take what you learn to create gains. A fitting example of this is Mother Against Drunk Drivers. The founder of the agency was a mom who lost her child to drunk driving. She created an organization that could be a resource to help others. She did not allow her pain and grief to consume her. She retooled these emotions to create something good.

Our lives are not our plans but the plans of the Lord. Before I was a thought or formed in the womb, God knew me. He already had plans for me, just as he had plans for my brother. I must understand that my brother's death was God's plan. I could not change what occurred. I had to accept his death and move on. God's plan was for me to wake up and live a life that is purposeful.

The story of John O'Leary is another powerful example of how one must move past pain. His pain ignited him to live. John was nine years old, playing with matches. One hundred percent of his body was burned, and he was given a 1 percent chance to live. To live, he had to fight through his pain. He spent five and half months in the hospital. The prognosis of him surviving was doubtful. However, survive he did—and more. Choosing to fight, John turned his pain into a resource to help and aid others. He is a speaker, author, and podcaster. He launched Rising Above to share his story and assure others that it is possible to rise above the trauma and storms in life.

I had to move on with my life and become the person needed for this world. Wallowing in pity and sadness was not going to bring back my brother. It was not going to change the situation. The spark of my brother was gone. His light had been extinguished.

There was still a plan for my life. I had to move forward to embrace this plan. But moving forward did not mean settling. We must make conscious decisions that align with what we are striving to achieve, living to make the vision planted in us by the Spirit a reality.

As Proverbs 29:18 states "Where there is no revelation, people cast off restraint; but blessed is the one heeds wisdom's instruction." The Spirit is our aid in vision casting. He empowers us to embrace and bring a vision to fruition.

Chapter 5
DETOUR ADDS TO CHARACTER

What is to give light must endure burning.
— Viktor Frankl, Man's Search for Meaning

I was lonely and tired until I met my first husband. We were high school classmates and made a connection at our twenty-year reunion. He asked me out on a date. We reminisced about high school days, even though we never ran in the same circles. It was ironic that after twenty years, we decided to take another look at each other.

He owned a home remodeling business and largely did projects for a woman who had him rehab properties she purchased. He also was a massage therapist. His passion was to own a salon. I already owned a business, so we shared that entrepreneurial passion. I saw our connection as predestined. High school years had not been the time for us to connect. But it was now our time. Now, we were inseparable.

I was enamored with him, thinking he was someone I could grow and build with. Instead, he was a person in bondage to emotional pain, obsessive thoughts, and compulsions that were holding him back. He was not free to become the person God created him to be. I could not free him. He had to free himself.

I had stars in my eyes, blinded to his true character. I failed to look under the surface to see a man who was wounded and suffering from low self-esteem. He did not believe in what he could do or become. I pressed forward, believing that we could become a unit, sharpening one another as iron sharpens iron.

We traveled to Las Vegas to elope. On the day we left, God attempted to stop me five times. Each time I was hindered in getting on the road, I said, "This is nothing but the devil."

I told myself, "God has blessed us to be together. He is a man of faith, active in his church. He is stable and appears to have a steady job and a home. I could not have asked for more."

What I saw with my eyes was not reality. I missed a lot.

We got married in May 2011. Our honeymoon was a horrible, unforgettable memory. My husband had me cowering in the hotel room. I was bawling my eyes out, crying so much I could have created a small pond. He made me believe I was a horrible person—that our union was not going to work and that I was going to bring him unhappiness. He said I was not faithful and that I had to turn from my wicked ways.

His behavior started when I recieved a phone call from a male coworker—who did not know I was on my honeymoon—about work. How would my coworker have known my husband and I had just eloped? My husband went through the roof. He accused me of cheating on him and stated that I was not the woman for him. I believed the words he was saying, and I felt defeated. If he felt this way, I thought, I had to change to prevent his insecurities. In reality, there was nothing I could have done to prevent his insecurity.

It did not get any better. Episodes such as this continued and escalated. The accusations and insecurities got worse. Our arguments continued with me being accused of cheating on him. He questioned everything I did. If I came home late, if I received a phone call—all these led to accusations of unfaithfulness. It got to be overwhelming.

We had no foundation. We had no pillar. God was not in our marriage. There was no getting better in this relationship. We had reached the pinnacle of our relationship before the marriage even began. I failed to see that this man was for a season, not a lifetime. He was not in God's plan for me.

Life is a journey filled with crossroads, and the choices we make at these crossroads have the power to shape our trajectory. Some choices propel us forward, igniting progress and growth, while others lead to stagnation, keeping us trapped in the status quo. Staying where you are will result in missed opportunities and unused potential.

In 2 Kings 7:3–20, four Samarian men afflicted with leprosy were were faced with a crossroad. The Aramean army was surrounding Samaria, but since the men were diseased, they were already outcast from the city. Knowing they were otherwise doomed to starve on the outskirts, they risked venturing into the enemy's camp to see if they could find food. They said to each other, "Why stay here until we die?" (2 Kings 7:3).

But when they arrived, they saw that God had been at work clearing a path for the Samarians. He had caused the Arameans to flee, abandoning their food and supplies. The four men with leprosy found the camp deserted and were able to announce to Samaria that God had lifted the siege and saved the city.

In a desperate moment, the men chose to move forward rather than resigning to their fate. Their leprosy was not taken away; however, they no longer faced death. They did find the resources they needed to survive. But these men did not only save themselves. Because they acted rather than resigning to their fate, they got to play a key role as God saved the entire city of Samaria.

Failing to take action is a decision. It is a decision for inaction. Inaction is complacency, unbelief, and hopelessness—it is turning your back on what can be. You must have faith in what can be achieved. Staying where you are will not result in your desired outcomes.

The lepers' affliction remained to keep them humble and focused on their purpose. Afflictions can fuel strength rather than weakness. In the face of adversity, you discover depths of courage and resilience that you never knew existed within you. It is through overcoming life's greatest challenges that you cultivate the inner fortitude to weather any storm.

Do not view afflictions as burdens that weigh you down; instead, shift your perspective to see them as catalysts for growth and resilience. Resilience isn't born out of weakness. It is forged in the fires of adversity. Afflictions teach invaluable lessons about perseverance, gratitude, and the power of the human spirit. They empower you to rise above life's challenges become better.

Just as a diamond is formed under intense pressure, you too are you shaped and strengthened by the adversities you face. Use adversity to move forward. Do not stay where you are. You must move. Make the decisions toward thriving.

Moving is difficult. It signifies closure. With my husband, I found it difficult to let go. But I would have to move to go forward.

SEE IN THE WORD

During my tumultuous marriage, my bond with God became stronger. I developed the daily habit of reading the Bible and praying. I would start my day at 4:30 a.m., reading and praying in God's Word. This laid the foundation for my day. I asked God to show me how I could apply the messages to my life. I wanted a deeper understanding of his Word. I began meditating on and internalizing it, chewing on it to get the full flavor and nourishment.

I was striving to understand the meaning of the scripture. I wanted to be like the person described in Psalm 1:2, "whose delight is in the law of the Lord, and who meditates on his law day and night." I would always ask, "What does it mean?" I examined each passage so I could savor it, experience its effect in my heart, and fill myself with peace and joy.

Whenever I did this, God provided me with the message. He revealed the meaning to equip me for the struggles and storms of the day. His word became my armor and my shield against the adversity I faced in my life, my marriage, and my career. His Word helped me keep pressing forward without being weighed down by what I endured during the day, nor by depression and distress. His Word became my lifeline, fulfilling me and providing contentment. I came to crave it. I let it dwell within me, so I could be unshaken—"rooted and built up in him, strengthened in the faith" (Colossians 2:7).

As God provided me with the application behind His Word, I had a strong desire to share his message. I wanted to share my delight. I thought I could help my husband. I began sharing my messages with him. Then God said, "Go further." I moved from sharing with him to sharing with family and friends. God placed a cause within me: inspire and motivate others through his Word. Because of him, I started writing a daily message to about fifteen individuals. Family and friends were grateful for the messages.

A friend once asked me, "Who's the author of the messages you send us?"

I replied, "Me."

The messages were the start of finally finding the God's for me.

Make That Move

My husband lost his job during the first six months of our marriage, so I became the primary breadwinner in the home. His job loss further impacted his mental state. He already had low self-esteem, but now, he was defeated and lacked direction as well. He desired to become an entrepreneur; however, he lacked focus, commitment, and dedication. The behavior I experienced from him on our honeymoon continued, and it only got worse.

My husband would go out until the wee hours of the morning, sometimes coming home when it was time for me to go to work. I would attempt to reach him while he was out, but he would not answer the phone. When questioned, he would give some lame excuse: battery died, he was in a bad cell area—things like that. We had fights like my parents did, fights that became physical. There were times when I was afraid for my life. I was fearful when he became angry because his anger was like an explosion. It was not uncommon for him to break something in the house. I saw my parents' marriage in my own. Deep inside, I was dying.

I recall one argument where he stated, "I cannot break you."

I looked at him. I was speechless. I said, "Why would you want to break me?"

I did not receive an answer.

When my husband and I would argue, I sought God. I would lock myself in the bathroom, praying, reading, and meditating. I asked God to change me, to make me into a better wife. I was reading scriptures to keep me going but, I was still not going in the right direction. I was trying to see what I was doing wrong. I would ask, "How could I be a better wife? What am I lacking?" But my request to God was missing the mark. God hit the pause button, waiting on me.

I eventually found the answers to my questions in my time with God. In the time I spent mediating and reflecting, God was talking to me. But I did not want to listen. I was fearful of taking a next step that would be life-changing. It was uncomfortable and scary. In my physical sight, I saw the next step as failing—failing and not being able to get back up.

ACTION IS REQUIRED

On my commute to work, my husband would call me to initiate an argument. I would get to work angry, unfocused, and flustered. After these instances, it always took a moment to get my bearings so I could be productive at work, doing what I was hired to do. I had to adopt the philosophy that you cannot allow one situation to impact another.

I recall a story that a father told a young boy. Each day as the father walked into the home, he would act as if there was a hook outside the door. As he walked into the house, he would pretend to hang up his coat.

The young boy asked the father, "What are you doing?"

The father answered, "I am leaving my worries and troubles of the day outside on this hook. I am hanging them up. What has happened to me outside in the world will not impact how I treat or interact with my family."

I have learned to live my life by these words. You cannot allow one situation to impact another or dictate how you treat others. I was determined to not allow my family life to impact how I treated those at my job. I suffered and endured in silence.

My life was spiraling out of control. The health club became my sanctuary. I would pound out my anger and hostility on the weights and through my cardiovascular workout. I had a regular routine. I would spend two and a half hours in the gym, weight training for about one hour and doing cardio for one and a half hours. I was dedicated to working out at least four days a week. It was my life jacket in turbulent waters. I was physically well but an emotional and social wreck.

As I exercised my body, I worked on getting spiritually fit as well. The spiritual sphere of my life became the foundation for the other spheres. A relationship and connection with God provided the framework I needed to address my emotional wounds and social challenges. I came to trust in God's timing and plan and find peace in his presence. I started to view myself through his eyes and navigate my emotional challenges with faith and wisdom. But this type of trust took me four years to understand and lean into.

For almost four years, I tried to endure, thinking it would get better, until the Spirit said, "This is enough." I was not created to live a life that was miserable. I was better than this. This marriage was draining me, and something had to change. God had spoken.

My eyes were looking at a man who was lost and needed help. The Spirit said, "You are not the one to help. This is not your cross to bear. This is not your assignment. It is time to move on."

I resisted this voice for as long as I could, until I realized it was only getting worse. The fights became even more frequent. I increasingly feared for my safety.

I had been looking at my husband with my physical eyes, and my eyes saw a man who had potential. But the Spirit saw it was not my potential to uncover. I needed to focus on my own purpose and potential. God had plans for me. I finally listened, and we separated. Even during the separation, I still clung to a glimmer of hope. We were not officially divorced, so I thought there was still a possibility of reconciling and restoring our marriage. However, I had to come to the realization that this was not a union God brought together, nor was it one with God in the center.

One evening during our period of separation, I attended a Tuesday night Bible study at Victory Apostolic Church. The pastor opened the doors of the church, and I jumped out of my seat as if I was on fire. I walked down the aisle to accept Jesus as my savior. My marriage had made me thirsty to deepen my relationship with God. The time had come to take our relationship to the next level.

That evening, I was baptized. Being baptized was a major turning point in my life. God had given me sight understand the scriptures. It was time for me to make my commitment to him—to be obedient, following him and serving. I attended my new church home with vigor, showing up to each Sunday service and Bible study on Tuesdays.

For about six weeks, my pastor conducted a Bible study series on 2 Corinthians. One night, we studied 2 Corinthians 6:14, which says, "Do not be yoked together with unbelievers. For what do righteousness and wickedness have in common? Or what fellowship can light have with darkness?"

This scripture punched me right in the face. God was talking to me. God does hate divorce; however, divorce is acceptable in some circumstances. I had yoked myself to someone who was not in alignment with my values and beliefs. I did not have a partnership or bond with my husband. We were two people who were cohabitating but who had no common purpose or foundation. We were merely roommates. Our marriage did not have God at the foundation. Ecclesiastes 4:12 says that "A cord of three strands is not quickly broken," but we were missing the third strand.

Our marriage was broken before it had begun, and I was trying to keep together that which had no foundation. It was time for me to let go of what was not present. I had to end this marriage to move forward in following God's plans for me—plans that were being held up by a marriage that was dead, a marriage that was going to be the death of me.

God directed me to another scripture: "Therefore what God has joined together, let no one separate" (Matthew 19:6). Through this scripture, God reminded me again that he did not bring me and my husband together. Our union was of my making. He had me revisit the day that we began our trip to Las Vegas to elope. God said, "I tried to stop you five times from going and taking this action. You would not listen. Instead, you kept going forward, not paying attention to my attempts to stop you. You had to learn your lesson. You have come around, and now you can see what I have been trying to get you to see for the past four years." God had been saying to me, "My daughter, follow me."

I had come to see that instead of looking to a man to aid me in my grief over my brother, I should have been looking to God. God is always the only answer. I made the mistake of seeing my husband as my savior when my savior was already with me. He was waiting on me to wake up and take the next step—to walk down the aisle and get baptized, committing and dedicating my life to Him. I found peace and comfort. I could move on.

Lean into him. He will heal and bring you through your pain. He will show you the way to go.

SEE THE ROCK

Because of my marriage, I found God and a church home. I found a place where I could grow and receive aid in seeing with the Spirit. I lost one relationship to gain a relationship that is everlasting. I gained a relationship with God.

In hindsight, I see God was always present. He had been attempting to get my attention. He had been walking with me. There were times that he carried me. During the fights, he had secured me under his wings, enabling me to endure. He kept me safe. I had been striving to attach to a man when I should have tethered myself to God, seeking God for comfort, clarity, and joy, uncovering what he is to me.

As I reflect on this period in my life, I saw how the death of my brother left a void in my life that I sought to fill with a man. I was lost, just drifting because I had lost a family member who was vital in my life. I was consumed with grief that clouded my vision.

I could not see past my pain.

Instead of looking to God, I looked to man for a replacement. I felt incomplete and abandoned, which led me to settle for bad treatment and for someone who was not for me. My pain obscured my judgment and caused me to see a man how I wanted to see him and not how God had intended. I tried to make the man into someone he was not.

I was playing the soundtracks: "I need someone to replace the one I lost. With time, this union will get better. This too shall pass. I must press forward to win the prize."

I replaced these soundtracks with affirmations to reaffirm my worth and purpose: "I will not be devalued. My value is priceless." "I want to live out my purpose." "Give the controls to God." "I am deserving of the life I have been gifted." "Go on and walk out the door. You are not welcome here anymore." These affirmations served as my guiding principles, reminding me to stand firm in my value, pursue my purpose, surrender to God's plan, embrace the life I deserve, and let go of anything that no longer served me. They empowered me to overcome negative thoughts and embrace a mindset of positivity, self-worth, and divine guidance.

Leaning into my physical sight had caused me to make a rash decision. This decision only extended my period of pain and grief. However, I have found the rainbow after my pain and grief: the Lord Jesus. I could see God and be well in him, not well with the man. With God, there is always peace and joy. No matter the storm that is raging, seek solace in him and you will be able to endure. Enduring does not mean there will be no pain and suffering. Enduring means that you will get through.

The Lord is my rock. God is described as a rock multiple times in scripture. Isaiah 26:3–4 says, "[God] will keep in perfect peace those whose minds are steadfast, because they trust in you. Trust in the Lord forever, for the Lord, the Lord himself, is the Rock eternal." Psalm 18:2 states, "The Lord is my rock, my fortress and my deliverer; my God is my rock, in whom I take refuge, my shield and the horn of my salvation, my stronghold."

Cling to the rock, and all will be well. When the world is raging around you, he is the rock that will enable you to withstand the raging waves and pummeling of the wind. He is the rock that provides solace and protection.

I took a detour that added to my character. I had temporarily lost my way in the grief and pain, causing me to look at only what I could see instead of looking within and to the source. With this lesson, I could get back on the path to my plan.

Chapter 6
SEE HOPE AND A FUTURE

It is time to embrace the cards you've been dealt with. Play your hand.

– Eric Thomas

Being separated from my first husband required me to take a long look at myself and the person I had become over the last four years. I had become a crutch for him. He was a crutch to me. I made excuses for his bad behavior. I accepted his temper tantrums. I held my tongue to keep arguments at bay because I was fearful of the outcome if they escalated. After the fights were over, I believed all would be well. Every time, I would say it was the last time. I was lonely and depressed.

However, the *real* last time was when God said to me, "The next time, it will be your head. You have to make a change today." I listened and made the change. I had created a challenging hand for myself. I had to play my cards strategically, using my resilience as my trump card to transform my circumstances and reclaim my power.

As I saw my situation clearly now, I saw that I had settled. I had selected an individual when my vision was clouded by my feelings. What I did was exchange one pain for another. In the absence of my husband, I had to come to grips with the passing of my brother and accept that he was gone all over again. Once again, I had to accept that there was nothing I could have done. The life I had envisioned was not to be. My plan was not God's plan. He has a plan for our lives that is different than the visions we create when we are not connected to Him.

In John 3:1–6, Jesus and a Pharisee named Nicodemus were having a discussion on being born again. Jesus said to him, "Very truly I tell you, no one can see the kingdom of God unless they are born again."

On the night that I was baptized, I was born again. I saw God. I was filled with his presence. He had set me free to live my life so I could see as He sees. I was released from the pain and grief so I could move on. I had to let go of the past to embrace a new future. I had to let go of the person who filled the void created by the loss of my brother.

God makes you complete and whole. He is forever present and available. With him, there is peace and joy even amid pain because he provides comfort and solace. On the night I was baptized, I buried the old me so the new me could emerge. I moved on with my life, embracing each day knowing God was with me. He is my provider.

There was a plan for me. I just had to get with the plan.

H. S. JACKSON

The Lesson

Selecting a mate is a process. You are seeking a partner that will last for a lifetime. You want someone who you can learn with and from, someone you can plant seeds with—seeds that will yield an abundant, significant, and impactful harvest. I am not speaking of material things; I am speaking of the intangible outcomes: peace, joy, happiness, and fulfillment. These are things that cannot be purchased. Look for these in the person you seek to spend a lifetime with. This person must be happy with themselves in order to share their self.

A union of two people should yield more than what one can accomplish alone. This is what I came to understand and realize. In my first marriage, there was no harvest. We were not moving forward in planting seeds. We were the weeds. We were choking the crop.

Look for someone who is like-minded and evenly yoked with you, sharing your values and beliefs. My first husband was an imposter. The Lord did not know him, and he did not know the Lord.

His relationship to God was like the story of the visitor at a church. The visitor came to the church as-is. The congregation looked down on the visitor because of the way the he was dressed. The visitor asked the pastor if they knew Jesus.

The pastor replied, "Yes, I am very familiar with him. We are close. Best buds."

The visitor responded, "Interesting, I spoke to him. He said he does not know you. He has not been to this church yet."

Likewise, my husband talked a good game, but the Lord had not visited him either. His display of faith was a façade.

When you are at your lowest point in life, your mind is unclear—do not make rash decisions. Find solace and comfort in the Spirit. I decided to marry my husband as my pain sought comfort. Find comfort instead in the one who is always available and present. While my husband was smooth talking to cover up his insecurities and weaknesses, I focused on what was being said, I failed to notice what was not being said. I failed to look beyond the physical appearance in order to see within.

The outward appearance will fool you. My husband was like Saul, the first king of the Israelites. Saul had a nice outward appearance, but inside he was a mess. Saul lacked courage, and his inner self was his weakness. What is within makes the person beautiful, not their looks.

Like Saul, my husband suffered from low self-esteem, and his inner self was his Achilles heel. He did not have the drive to get past the setbacks in his life. "No" made him stop and give up on becoming who he could be. He was wounded, suffering from the disappointment of not being successful in his business or career. His disappointment degraded his self-confidence and self-image instead of kicking his butt into gear to work for the things he wanted. A person who is confident, passionate, and visionary has the courage to pursue what they want and not give up. Instead of putting forth the effort to create opportunities that helped realize his vision, he wanted handouts. He had given up.

Due to his frustrations with himself, he lashed out at those around him—primarily me. He wanted me to be his punching bag, to be complacent, and to give him all I had. He expected me to let go of my identity and let him overshadow and overpower me. I had to decrease for him to increase. He sought to oppress me instead of uplifting me.

It is important when choosing a soulmate that you get to

know the person that is to become one with you. Understand their foundation, beliefs, and values. See beyond the outer shell—the vessel of clay. Get clarity on how the two of you align and complement one another. Pay attention to the person's actions. Actions speak louder than words. Listen to what is being said and what is not said. Take the time to establish a connection and communicate. These are all the things I failed to do in my first marriage.

Fresh Start

I met David Jackson one day at the gym. We were both working out. He jumped on my machine while I had turned my back for a second. (He tells a different story.) We exchanged numbers. He did not call me; I called him.

We planned a date that did not happen as intended, as he got tied up at a baseball game with his son. David contacted me to let me know he was delayed after I had already arrived at the restaurant. As far as I was concerned, he had struck out. I was done. Because he was a no-show, I decided that he had missed his chance. I was not going to fall for another façade, as I had done with my first husband. I had learned my lesson and was now paying attention to all signs.

However, David called me about two or three more times attempting to connect again after missing our first date. I blew him off.

God said to me, "Daughter, give him another chance. Can you not see that he is trying to make amends? Give him another chance as I done for you."

I listened to God and gave David another chance. It was a very nice first date. He had such a bright spirit. I was looking to see the person within him. He was shy and a perfect gentleman. He opened my door to the car and to the restaurant. He was very attentive. As we continued to date, I got to know him. I found him to be kind, loving, and compassionate. He was sensitive and caring. He loved the Lord—and still does.

His story is not mine to share. He has been through trials and storms in this life that he would not have been able to withstand if it had not been for God's mercy, love, and grace. David gets emotional and choked up about his past.

He was able to recover because of God. God showed him love. Based on love, he had hope for a better future and way of life. David turned his life around.

He loves his son, who is his priority. David did not make our first date because of his dedication to his son. He wanted to make sure his son got to play sports and experience life with all the opportunities to play as a child should.

David's actions mirrored his words. He walked his talk.

We took the time to get to know each other. David's philosophy is that you must first be friends. If there is no friendship, there is no foundation. I concur with and respect this philosophy. As we grew in friendship, we found similarities and differences that complemented one another. As we spent time together, we connected beyond the physical to a deeper understanding of each other's thoughts and emotions, creating a bond that felt both profound and transformative.

In making my decision to marry David, I asked God for his blessing. I asked God if this union was of his making. I spent time with God, being quiet and letting him talk to me. I did not want to repeat the same nightmare from which I had escaped.

God said to me, "My child, this one is for you."

I smiled and thanked him for the blessing. I wanted our wedding day to reflect his blessing. I desired to look up and see him smiling down upon our union.

I married David Jackson on August 26, 2017. This was one of the happiest days of my life. The ceremony was held at a local venue, presided over by my pastor. The day of our wedding was a perfect summer day. There was not a cloud in the sky. I looked up, and I saw God. I saw him smiling. He promised I would have joy, peace, happiness, and fulfillment.

God was first in our lives as he would be first in our marriage. With him as a foundation, we were ready to build a home that would withstand the storms and challenges to come. Together we knew nothing is impossible with God. We wanted to live in alignment with God's purpose, striving to be in joy and peace in all aspects of life. We knew the Spirit would be our guide to wellness in God. Spiritual wellness enabled us to accept what we couldn't control and give it to God. We trusted and believed in him, having faith in the "knowing" of the Spirit. This union showed me the hope and the future that God had promised me.

In David, I finally found a partner. Marriage is a partnership which joins man and woman to be supportive of each other as each lives out the purpose of their lives. Mark 6:7 states "[Jesus] began to send them out two by two." This simple yet profound statement holds a truth that resonates across cultures and generations: there is strength in partnership. There is power in collaborating.

Throughout history, humans have recognized the power of partnership. Whether embarking on a physical journey, facing a daunting task, or simply navigating the ups and downs of life, having someone by your side can make all the difference. Jesus highlights the wisdom of this approach. He understood the importance of sending his disciples out in pairs.

The concept of "two by two" extends far beyond its literal interpretation. It speaks to the inherent value of community, collaboration, and mutual support. Being in the company of another, you not only have someone to share your burdens and joys but also someone to lean on in times of need.

There are three key benefits of being in a partnership.

1. The exchange of strength: In moments of weakness, the other person can offer encouragement and support, helping you find the inner resilience to persevere. Likewise, you have the opportunity to uplift and empower the other person when they face challenges. Together, you and the other person become stronger than the sum of your parts.

2. Learning and growth: Through meaningful interactions and shared experiences, you gain new perspectives, insights, and skills. The other person possesses knowledge or abilities that complement your own, enabling you to learn from each other and expand your horizons.

3. Security and belonging: Knowing that someone cares for you unconditionally and has your back fosters a deep sense of trust and connection. This emotional support bolsters your confidence and resilience, allowing you to navigate life's uncertainties with greater ease.

The message of "two by two" reminds you of the importance of cultivating meaningful relationships and embracing the power of community. Whether in times of triumph or adversity, having someone to share the journey with enriches your life and enhances your wellbeing.

I Am Complete

I uncovered the key to true wellness: being in harmony in mind, body, and spirit and being in alignment with God's purpose. Wellness begins with being anchored to a foundation that can withstand the storms of life.

We can have peace and joy knowing that there is security and safety under God's wings. Psalm 91:4 states, "He will cover you with his feathers, and under his wings you will find refuge; his faithfulness will be your shield and rampart." Under his wings, you cannot see, which means that you must trust in him to provide safety, security, hope, and love. To be covered with God's feathers and find refuge under his wings is to experience an intimate and personal safety. Just as a bird shelters its young under its wings, God's protection is close, encompassing, and reliable.

What does it mean to find refuge under His wings? How does this relate to your daily life? There are three applications.

1. Developing deep personal trust: Being hidden under God's wings means you are completely shielded from the outside world. Resting under God's wings means placing your trust in him to provide safety and security. This requires faith to sustain you in those periods when tangible assurance is absent. It means leaning on God's promises and character even when the path ahead is unclear.

2. Surrendering fears and anxieties: In a world full of uncertainties and challenges, the assurance of God's protection can be a source of great comfort. Trusting in his wings means relinquishing our own attempts to control every situation and accepting that his plan is sovereign and perfect. It is

about acknowledging that, though we cannot always see or understand what God is doing, his faithfulness remains our constant shield and rampart.

3. Having hope and love: God's protection is not merely about shielding us from harm but also about nurturing us with his love and care. His wings represent his steadfast love and commitment to our wellbeing. By trusting in his protective embrace, we open ourselves to experiencing his profound love and the hope he offers even in difficulties.

Finding refuge under God's wings requires us to trust, surrender, and having hope and love in conjunction with prayer and meditation on his Word. Practicing these disciplines will position you to seek his guidance. Making conscious choices to trust him with your concerns will allow you to find peace in his promises.

Under God's wings, you are safe and secure. His faithfulness is your shield and rampart, providing unwavering protection and an unshakable foundation of hope and love. Trusting in his shelter means embracing the assurance that you are never alone and are always cared for in his divine embrace.

I am united with something that is bigger than me. I am not living for what I want but striving to live for who created me. When I made this shift, I was no longer fragmented. I could breathe. I could see that my life was on a new path. I had endured the hardship and trial of losing both my parents and my best friend (my brother). I had withstood an abusive and hostile marriage for four years. I had persevered. I had gained so much.

I had lost my birth father but was now united with the spiritual Father. And I found my best friend, David. I had lost multiple people, but I had also gained.

What is ironic is that I was never alone. God was present with me the entire time from the moment I was born. I was the one who had been lost. It took the desert for me to find him, just as he had been with the Israelites for the forty years they wandered the desert. Not once had their clothes or shoes worn out. They had not lacked sustenance. God provided food and water. As with them, I had lacked for nothing. I had suffered loss and experienced heartache. I had lost family members and finances. However, I made it through. There were lessons I needed to learn to become the person my life's plan needed me to be.

Lessons From the Detour

Once you stop looking at the place you want to be and instead accept the place where you are, you can see there are benefits to the detours you have taken. I came to realize that I recieved seven benefits from my desert.

Benefit #1: I faced and resolved negative emotions. When my brother passed, my inner voice kept saying I could have saved him. This soundtrack continued to play in my head, leading me to think negatively about myself. However, I learned to shut down this negative soundtrack and replace it with the affirmation that God is in control.

Benefit #2: My desert uncovered my unhealthy habits. I had stopped reading and instead picked up the habit of watching television excessively. I realized the importance of balancing my leisure time with productive activities like reading, volunteering, and taking courses.

Benefit #3: My desert revealed the drawbacks of relying solely on physical sight. In Mark 10:46–52 there was a blind beggar, Bartimaeus. He could not physically see Jesus; however, his spirit saw Jesus, who he was, and what he could do. Bartimaeus called out, "Son of David, have mercy on me!"

The people sought to silence Bartimaeus, but he would not be silenced. He kept going; he said, "Rabbi, I want to see." And see he did. Instantly, he was healed, and his sight was restored.

However, Bartimaeus had sight all along—just not physical sight. Imagine if Bartimaeus had listened to others and stopped calling to Jesus, stopped pressing forward to get to him. He would have missed out on being able to see physically. Instead, his spirit kept him going. His spirit knew and believed what was possible.

I learned from the story of Bartimaeus that spiritual sight empowers us to believe in what is possible, even when physical sight fails us. My spirit can see while my physical sight is hindered. My desert revealed that I had used my physical sight to select my first husband and the business that was not for me. God had delivered—these were all in the past. I had to move on. I had a future. I needed see and believe in that future. I had a life to live. I had a purpose that I needed to find and follow.

Benefit #4: I found that many of the barriers I faced were onesthat I had created myself. I learned that while there may be obstacles, there is always another way forward.

Benefit #5: My desert provided solitude for reflection and introspection. I learned the importance of being still and quiet to hear the voice of God and gain insight for myself.

Benefit #6: I had time to strategize and plan. I came to understand the importance of developing a clear course of action to achieve my goals.

Benefit #7: My desert built a stronger bond with the Source. I realized that God is always available and ready to establish a relationship with us; it is up to us to reach out to him.

My desert experience was not wasted; it taught me invaluable lessons and led to personal growth and spiritual development. I learned what it means to be well in him.

In 2 Kings 4:18–37, a Shunammite woman who had been baren was blessed to birth a son. The son became ill and died. She left her house to go find the prophet Elisha. When her husband questions her, she responds, "That's all right."

Elisha sees her coming and sends his servant to greet her. The servant asks how she and her husband and son are. The Shunammite woman responds, "Everything is all right."

The woman spoke these words with her son lying dead on his bed—a son she was blessed to have when she had no hope of ever having a child. Within, she is in turmoil; however, the words she speaks say the opposite .

This woman's words are a profound expression of faith and trust in God even in the face of a personal tragedy. Despite the death of her son, she maintains a sense of peace and acceptance.

She is able to speak these words because of her faith. She has reassurance, comfort, and acceptance of what occurred. She conveys a sense of peace, contentment, and resolution in the face of challenges or difficult situations.

She believes everything will ultimately be okay, and she is right. God blesses Elisha with the power to revive her son. He is returned from death.

Know that in your challenges, you will be well. God is with you.

Say these three words to yourself: "It is well." They will propel you forward to overcome and conquer your situation. With God, you will recover, and all will be okay. It is God's will that is done and not yours. Be well in him, for it is well.

Being well in him changed my perspective on my desert so I could see benefits instead of drawbacks. The seven benefits revealed to me that the desert is for good and not intended for harm. The desert is necessary to see yourself and get clarity. You must know who you are and where you are to go. The desert makes you stronger.

Do not attempt to run from the desert. Running will only make it harder. The pain will only become more overwhelming. You are running against the current that is taking you on the course of your life. Stop fighting so you can see what you must see to move forward. See the desert as an opportunity. Gain understanding and knowledge from what you encounter in that desolate place. The desert enables you to find the way that you must go.

The desert allowed me to reframe my outlook. I no longer looked at my situations with pain. I was able to see the world as God sees, not as what I see. I could finally see past the pain to view what God needed me to understand.

Jesus endured and suffered for me. He had the choice not to follow the path of the Father; however, he chose to continue moving forward. Pain and suffering are part of the process. Yes, it is hard, but it cannot be avoided. It pains God to see the sinfulness of mankind, but he does not give up on us. Just like God, I cannot give up on my life because of my pain and suffering. I must believe and trust in him, following the plans he has for me.

Recall that Jesus was in the wilderness for forty days and nights to face the ultimate test of endurance. Deprived of food and water, he withstood the relentless hounding of the devil, who sought to lure him away from God's path.

The climax of this spiritual battle occurred as the devil made one final attempt, taking Jesus to a high mountain to offer him all the world's riches in exchange for his allegiance. Jesus remained steadfast, firmly rejecting the devil's temptations. In Matthew 4:9, he commands, "Away from me, Satan! For it is written: 'Worship the Lord your God, and serve him only.'"

In this pivotal moment, the devil presented Jesus with the allure of an "easy route"—a shortcut to avoiding adversity and challenges to come. Jesus refused to compromise his values and beliefs, choosing instead to remain faithful to his purpose. His unwavering commitment serves as a powerful example. Embrace life's challenges and adversities as opportunities for growth and transformation.

Just as Jesus endured the trials of the wilderness for the greater good, so too must you navigate the vicissitudes of life with courage and perseverance. You must stay true to your values and beliefs in the face of temptation. You will emerge stronger and more resilient, fulfilling the purpose God has set before you. Draw inspiration from Jesus' example, trusting in God's plan for your life. Find hope and redemption in adversity. Move through the hardships to live in the purpose of your life.

Chapter 7
VISUALIZE THE JOURNEY

Do not go where the path may lead, go instead where there is no path and leave a trail.

– RALPH WALDO EMERSON

In 2009, I traveled to Switzerland with a group of friends. The countryside was breathtaking. We made an excursion to the Matterhorn. With its nearly symmetrical, pyramidal peaks reaching 4,478 meters high, it creates the highest summits in the Alps and Europe. The journey to our destination took about three hours. We had to take a train to a certain point, get off, take another train, then get off that train to board a lift, which finally took us to the top of the mountain.

I will always have the memory of traveling on the train through the Swiss countryside. It was majestically beautiful with mountains, hills, waterfalls, streams, and rivers. Seeing the beauty of nature had me in awe. As I observed the scenery, my excitement increased. I was so enthralled with the scenery that I was not concerned with the time it took to travel to the Matterhorn. I was content with the journey. Yes, getting to the summit was the ultimate goal; however, it was the journey that made the trip. This is what I had to learn in my twenty-year career with a government agency.

For twenty years, I was employed in the federal government. It took me seventeen years to understand that I had missed the scenery. I was so focused on looking for someone to pave my path, yet I missed the truth that *I* was the someone who needed to pave the way. My sight was focused on the destination instead of appreciating the journey and understanding that each step I took was laying the foundation for my future in God. I was seeking to please man and not God. In Galatians, the Apostle Paul was speaking on living by human perspective versus living by God's perspective. I had spent seventeen of my twenty years of employment living by human perspective. I was focused on pleasing my supervisors and peers, making them proud of me. I was seeking to fit in. I was allowing my environment to set limits on my life, just like I had done in my childhood.

Life span development theories explore how individuals are shaped by their environment. In this way, I had regressed to what I had been taught as a child. I was again allowing my environment to place limits on my potential. I was empowering individuals to mold me into a forgotten person. You become forgotten by sitting in a corner because you've been told your thoughts and opinions don't matter. You walk in the shadows of others because you've been brainwashed to believe you're inferior. In both your personal or professional life, you fear taking the next steps to level up. You relinquish authority to others to make decisions for your life. Life's storms and crises put you in permanent pause, resulting in settling.

Does any one of these descriptions resonate with you? That is what I had become. Recall in *Dirty Dancing*, the star, Baby, walked in the shadow of her older sister, Lisa. Lisa was given preferential treatment by her father, Dr. Jake, who viewed her as the star of the family.

Dr. Jake put Baby in the corner. He lavished all his attention on Lisa. But the bad boy, Johnny, saw the potential in Baby. At first, he tried to ignore her as well, but Baby was a woman with talent. She was not created to be in the shadows, nor to be overlooked. In the final scene, Johnny walks up to Baby's table at the banquet. He tells her dad, "No one puts Baby in a corner."

Johnny takes Baby's hand, and they dance. They shake up the party and make a boring dance the highlight of the entire vacation. This is what I say to myself: "No one is going to put me in a corner. I will not be undervalued." I had to stand up and take action! I was not created to be devalued but to be significant and impactful. I had empowered others to place limits on me. I had failed to see beyond the people around me and my natural sight.

It took me seventeen of the twenty years to see that the years I spent miserable in my job were my own fault. The job had been my training ground. I had been so busy focusing on my emotions and other people that I suffered. I was lamenting over the people and environment, failing to see the experiences I had gained. For those seventeen years, I had developed my character, molding myself into the person I am today. The change brought on by the Coronavirus outbreak was the catalyst that shocked me out of my limitations. Being sheltered at home and working at home for almost two years gave me time to pause, reflect, think, and evaluate. This period enabled me to gain understanding. God had been teaching me.

Just like my journey to the mountain in Switzerland, my career had been my journey to develop and mature. I missed the journey because I was focused on my destination. I did not see that what occurred and what I endured was designed for me to understand my purpose. It took two years of being still and quiet in the pandemic to see that with clarity. I learned to stop focusing on my feelings so I could appreciate the scenery. The scenery was the lessons and experiences I had gained.

Like the journey to get to the top of the Matterhorn, my journey in this agency was intense. There were those in my group who turned back. My journey in particular was brutal. There were times when I wanted to give up. I was attacked by every supervisor because I was not a conformer. I stuck to my values and beliefs. People matter to me, and I opposed being part of any plans that devalued an individual. There were times when my journey was overwhelming because of the opposition. Still, I kept going, being resilient and courageous.

In the journey of life, there are moments when you may feel unsure, insecure, or even overwhelmed by the challenges that lie ahead. In times like these, finding solace in faith can provide immense strength and comfort.

One source of reassurance is found in the words of Philippians 1:6: "[Be] confident of this, that he who began a good work in you will carry it on to completion until the day of Christ Jesus." At first glance, this verse may seem simple, but its profound message resonates deeply with the human experience. It speaks to the notion of divine intervention and the belief that every individual is part of a greater plan. The assurance that the God who initiated a positive transformation within you will see it through to fruition is immensely comforting. Be is active. It involves awareness of thoughts, taking deliberate action aligned with values and a continual renewal of choices.

Life is a journey filled with ups, downs, twists, and turns. Along the way, we encounter numerous challenges, obstacles, and setbacks that may cause us to doubt our abilities or question our purpose. Philippians 1:6 reminds you to have faith in the process. Trust that the seeds of goodness planted within you will eventually blossom into something beautiful.

This verse highlights two key points:

1. It speaks to the concept of personal growth and development. Change is a gradual process, often requiring patience, perseverance, and resilience. Just as a seed takes time to sprout, grow, and bear fruit, so too do your talents, virtues, and inner strengths unfold over time.

2. It emphasizes the role of divine guidance and intervention in our lives. Your journey is not one you navigate alone but with the support and guidance of a higher power. This recognition can instill in us a sense of hope, purpose, and direction, especially during times of uncertainty or adversity.

Philippians 1:6 is a powerful reminder to have faith in oneself and in the divine plan unfolding within you. It encourages you to embrace the journey of self-discovery, growth, and transformation with confidence and optimism. Regardless of the challenges you face or the obstacles you encounter, take comfort in knowing that the one who initiated this journey within you will see it through to completion. Trust the process, have faith in the journey, and believe in the power of divine intervention to guide you toward your fullest potential.

Reflect On the Lessons

Looking back over my twenty-year career in the agency, I had a total of seven different supervisors. From each, I gained knowledge and experience.

Supervisor #1 was female. She moved up through the ranks of the Chicago Police Department (CPD) to become a high-ranking official. During her tenure at CPD, women in high-ranking positions were rare. She was tough but fair, honest, and trustworthy. She walked her talk. Her toughness was a result of her need to press forward and up the ranks in CPD. Hers are qualities I admire and have emulated.

I recall once when she attended a town hall meeting with a workforce of over seven hundred individuals. The workforce was complaining about the administrative staff. Their perception was that staff were not responding to their issues or serving their needs, but the workforce only saw one side of the equation. Staff were not able to respond because we lacked support from Headquarters to be able to address and resolve the issues. My supervisor immediately came to the rescue of her staff. She stated that her staff members were working their butts off trying to support the workforce and that they were doing their best. She stood up for her team. She was loyal, with strength, tenacity, and stamina.

Supervisor #2 was male. He was an introvert. He reported to work and stayed in his office. He made no attempts to get to know his staff. He did not walk around the office to establish connections or get to know what was in the hearts of his team members.

From this supervisor, I learned that you must walk the room and get to know the people who work for you. You must be available and accessible to your team and let them know they matter and are appreciated. Touching their hearts results in trust and loyalty.

Supervisor #3 was male. He worked his way up through the ranks as a front-line employee. He had an open-door policy, which I viewed as positive and negative: positive because it said, "I am approachable and care about you," but negative because it undermined the authority and power of his subordinates. My philosophy is that attempts to resolve conflicts should first be handled by the immediate supervisor. If there is no resolution, then move the issue up the leader ladder. When you empower individuals to circumvent others, it creates a hostile work environment. This practice also limits the growth of the manager or supervisor by not exposing them to conflict resolutions.

It turned out that while this supervisor claimed to value all people, he did not walk his talk. He valued the individuals he chose to value while treating others as less-than. For me, this reinforced the danger of making one person feel that they have power over another. I deepened in my belief in a level playing field. Each person's feelings are important. We must include everyone in the process from start to finish, not just in the middle or at the end.

In my time working under this supervisor, I applied for a promotion in which he was the deciding official. I did not believe I had a chance because, after witnessing his treatment of fellow staff members, I kept my distance. I made no attempts to be engaged or noticed. My mission was to get my work done and go home.

As I had expected, I was not selected. He chose an individual from another location, but she ultimately declined the reassignment since she lived out of state. Instead of reposting the position, my supervisor selected me as the runner up. I was selected because of God. God used this man to make the selection. God was moving me up the ladder to develop my skills as a leader. God was showing me the way by giving me more, as "more" is my motivator. God determined I was to be promoted and assigned. Know and believe that what God has for you, no man can stop. Look to God and not man.

Supervisor #4 was male. He was not humble nor open to listening. He had all the answers. He did not accept or incorporate the ideas of his team. To him, there was only one way. But that was a fallacy. There is always another way, though you may have elected to go only one way.

He showed me that a leader must be a spark that lights up their team, encouraging them and tapping into their potential. A leader is to inspire their team to grow and equip them with the resources to do so. He was not equipping anyone or promoting growth. He was placing limits on their thinking and creativity. A leader should not close their mind to other ways. There are many ways, and there is always a better way. Encourage your team to be creative, contributing to the mission and cause. Do not tie their hands and treat them as if they do not know what they are doing. Value each person and aid them in growing. A leader should empower and inspire his or her team to embrace growth.

Supervisor #5 was another male. He was a hermit, too. He made no attempt to communicate or connect with anyone. You would have thought the staff had a plague. If you passed him in hallway, he literally pressed himself to the wall to avoid any form of close contact. He was not a resident of the city or state, but he rented an apartment close by. He would fly into town on Monday morning, then depart by noon every Friday.

He was disengaged and hands-off. He relied on his second-in-command to handle and resolve daily operations. He avoided making decisions. If there was an issue, he would bury his head in the sand. An entire management team was claiming a hostile work environment had resulted from his second-in-command. My supervisor's mindset was that, eventually, it would all blow over. His perception of this second-in-command was clouded. He did not want to see the truth. His thought that subordinates and others on the team just needed to find ways to get along. He did not step in to resolve, correct, or address issues. Now, I don't know about you, but I think if an entire team of ten individuals are complaining about one individual, the person in charge should step in.

This supervisor taught me that you must lead. Leadership requires action. A leader does not sit in a seat holding a position, doing nothing. You must get involved with those on your team. A leader influences, looks to increase loyalty, and finds ways to uplift, not tear down. This supervisor's behavior and actions did not portray a leader. A leader listens, connects, and communicates. He did none of these things.

I also learned in this season that a leader must strive to make a difference. It is not about what I want but what I can do to aid others on my team. This supervisor was coasting along with only his selfish desires and plans in mind. He was only at this job for the paycheck. His mindset was focused on surviving, not thriving. His actions and behavior shouted, "I do not care."

Supervisor #6—another male. I vividly recall an incident in which he called a huddle with me, himself, and one of my team members who was also female. He had an issue with a comment she made. Although I was not present when the incident occurred, I thought it was good that he included me in the meeting, as it showed teamwork and collaboration.

The meeting started as he presented his perspective of the incident. My team member then gave her interpretation. While she explained her side, I watched my supervisor. At first, his face was open. He wore a slight smile, encouraging the conversation. But as my team member continued to talk, the smile disappeared. It reminded me of when someone is walking outside, and there is no warning of a thunderstorm. The sun is shining brightly when, suddenly, the sky darkens. I saw this occur in a person. A different person emerged in the meeting. The smile on his face was gone.

I tried to get my team member's attention to tell her to be quiet. I could not kick her because he would have seen me. I was stuck as she continued to talk.

Abruptly, he said, "I have had enough. You are to listen and not speak. You are to speak when I tell you to speak."

I know the look on my face was aghast. I immediately looked down because of his tone. How he said what he said was totally disrespectful, making me angry. My team member had tears in her eyes. I started praying to God to hold my tongue and to end this meeting as soon as possible. God answered my prayers to both. I immediately went to my office and shut the door. I had to regain my composure. This meeting showed me that my supervisor was not who I thought he was. I saw "STOP" in capital red letters. Going forward, I was watchful of this man.

After this incident, I began witnessing further inconsistencies in his behavior. He belittled a manager in a meeting, yelling and cursing at him. In one meeting, he attempted to be disrespectful to me. I was not having that. My face must have said so because he asked the others to leave the room. We had a discussion that did not end well for the two of us. This meeting set the tone for the remainder of our working relationship.

As I reflect on this supervisor, he helped me take the lid off my spiritual growth. I had to go deeper. I had developed the practice of praying before I left work. God had been revealing the messages in the scripture to me since my first marriage. I had to now embrace those messages to see the course I needed to pursue in my career.

As I read the scriptures, I asked myself: What does this mean to me? How does this affect me? What am I to learn? How can I apply it? God's word is the blueprint for your life. I had to go deeper to find my way and my purpose.

I began talking more about God at work, while being mindful not push my beliefs on others. I had many enlightening conversations with coworkers that helped me see how the message God gave me applied to my workplace and how it could help me find my way.

Lastly, Supervisor #7 was another male. He was dishonest and untrustworthy. I learned to let your words be your bond. Do not chase money. Money comes and goes. It is not everlasting. What is everlasting is what is within you.

I came to see patterns in each of my supervisors. I ask you to reflect on the patterns in your life. There is a lesson and reason to the patterns.

Sharpening

Proverbs 27:17 says, "As iron sharpens iron, so one person sharpens another." We tend to think that only individuals we admire or are close to you can sharpen us and aid in your development. This is not true. Individuals that lack skills can show you how not to be, too. I recall a meeting that I had with a supervisor.

He said to me, "I am trying to teach you."

I looked at him and said, "There is nothing you can teach me."

I was totally wrong. He taught me how not to be as a leader.

As I reflected upon these seven supervisors, I saw that I had grown tremendously. With each supervisor, I underwent pruning. I better understood what it meant to be a leader, coach, and mentor. What follows is what I have learned of being a leader.

First and foremost, a leader is a servant. One must first give a hand before asking for a hand. Jesus says it best when he proclaimed, "the Son of Man did not come to be served, but to serve, and to give his life as a ransom for many" (Matthew 20:28). As a leader over my department, I did not ask any team member to perform a task that I did not perform first. I did not believe that any task was beneath me.

Second, a leader is to be a coach and mentor and to assist others in getting what they want. If you help individuals get what they want, they will give you what you want. I was instrumental in promoting at least four team members from the front line to become administrative staff. Individuals have aspirations; it is the responsibility of a leader to facilitate those making aspirations a reality. I insisted that team members attend training. Growth and development are paramount. Once you stop learning, you will stop growing.

A leader must also be approachable. I had an open-door policy. Team members felt comfortable speaking to me about their issues, both personal and professional. I recall numerous conversations I held with team members in which I just listened. That is what they needed: someone to just be an ear.

Another essential quality is that a leader must adapt. I was open to new ways of thinking and new methodology. I was not stuck in my way as the only way. I explained what the outcome or solution would be, but it was the team members' responsibility to determine the methodology toward the solution.

A leader must be able to communicate. Connecting is identifying and relating to increase your influence. When you communicate the goal, you create a connection. When making a connection, you strive to create an experience that individuals will enjoy and remember. You want to be remembered. Connections are made with the heart using the tongue. The tongue communicates what is in your heart.

This is essential: a leader must have vision to see what others do not see. Look to the future and chart a new course. I saw the potential of each member. I placed team members in positions to aid them in becoming better and moving forward.

Lastly, a leader must know when to take the back seat as well, like with John the Baptist and Jesus. John paved the way for Jesus. Once Jesus arrived, he had to step back. As with me, my time with the agency had come to an end. The journey prepared me for the destination. It was time for me to step back so that I could move forward.

Embrace the Journey

I had endured my training for seventeen years. The time had come for me to plan my next move. I could not stay where I was and move forward. I had grown into a person who could help others to not be forgotten and to live lives of impact and significance.

I could not fall into the trap of waiting. In John 5:1–9, there is a man who had been crippled for thirty-eight years. For thirty-eight years, he had been suffering, feeling hopeless, waiting for someone to help him into the pool to be healed. Jesus walked up to the man, asking if he was ready to be well. The man made excuses, blaming others for his inaction. Jesus' immediate response was to direct the man to take initiative. Jesus said, "Get up! Pick up your mat and walk." He knew healing was available if the man took action to receive the healing. The man rose, no longer crippled.

Now, I felt he was saying the same to me: get up and walk. There were no excuses. I had to move. Just like this man. I had to stop looking to others to lead me. It was not their responsibility to take me by the hand. The responsibility belonged to me. I was in control. What I desired and sought required ownership and action.

It is easy to fall into the trap of waiting for someone else to take the lead—to be the guide for the path you want to travel. We may find ourselves looking to others for direction, reassurance, and validation. The truth is that you are responsible for your journey.

You are waiting for the perfect moment, the right opportunity, or the ideal circumstances before acting—hesitating and procrastinating because of fear. The reality is that there will never be a perfect moment. There will always be obstacles in the way, challenges to overcome, and risks to take. Waiting for everything to align perfectly will result in waiting forever.

There are three keys to breaking the trap:

1. The first key is leadership. You have the authority to shape your life according to your desires and aspirations. Be proactive, decisive, and assertive in the pursuit of goals.

2. The second key is self-awareness. Take the time to reflect on what you truly want out of life. Identify the steps needed to get there. Evaluate strengths, weaknesses, and areas for growth.
3. The third key is courage. Step outside of your comfort zones, take risks, and embrace the unknown. Silence the doubts and naysayers, both external and internal, and push forward.

Stop waiting for someone else to take the lead. No more excuses or procrastinating.

Move boldly toward the future you envision for yourself. You will discover that the power to shape your destiny has been within you all along.

Chapter 8
SEE IN THE QUIET PLACE

You don't have to see the whole staircase, just take the first step.

– Martin Luther King Jr.

Sometimes, we must become physically blind to gain sight. When we let go of the need to see every detail of our future path, we free ourselves to stop focusing on the entire staircase and instead take the first step. We must challenge reliance on physical sight, trust in the unseen, and move forward despite uncertainty.

Recall the story of Saul before he became the Apostle Paul. Saul was the ringleader among those persecuting Jesus' disciples. He had authorization from the high priest to capture any person who believed in Christ. In Acts 9, Saul was traveling to Damascus, full of himself. He was not open to seeing or believing in Christ.

Suddenly, Paul was blinded. Losing his sight and falling to the ground, he heard a voice ask him, "Saul, Saul, why do you persecute me?"

Saul answered, "Who are you, Lord?"

Saul's blindness was the turning point in his life. His physical sight had ruled his heart and mind. His physical sight told him that Jesus was not God. Afterall, Jesus looked just like Saul himself: a man with flesh and blood. God is not flesh, Saul may have reasoned. His eyes had developed an image of who and what God was supposed to be. His physical sight caused him to miss out on possibilities because his eyes had programmed his mind to see the Lord in only one way.

Not being able to see enabled Saul to find clarity as he thought and saw using his Spirit. He reviewed the evidence that he witnessed with his eyes but had not processed with his Spirit.

As with Saul, my sight caused my mind to become programmed with limited settings. Physical sight only allowed me to see one way. You cannot become stymied by seeing only what is physically visible. You must believe in a vision of what can be realized. It is achieved based on effort, dedication, faith, and hope.

Prior to the Coronavirus pandemic, I was a health club fanatic. I was committed to working out at the gym at least four days a week for about three hours each time. I had a set program. I would participate in the cycling class two to three days a week and perform weight training four days a week. I mixed cardio with weight training. When the virus first hit, David and I continued to go to the gym. We were cautious, but we had faith and hope. We knew we would survive.

The virus continued to rage on, causing the entire world to shut down. Countries were closing their borders to travelers in and out. On March 21, 2020, Governor Pritzker announced that the state of Illinois would go into a mandatory shelter-in-place. Residents were permitted to leave and return only for essential activities. My health club was shut down.

I wondered, what am I going to do? The health club had been my way of life for over thirty years. It was my place of solace and refuge, pushing me through my desert many times. It was my lifeline and antidote to combat the stress and anger of the world. It was my sanctuary, the place where I could pause, reflect, think, and strategize. This was where I had my time with God, replaying the day with him and seek his guidance.

I knew there had to be another way to do get the peace and processing time that I needed, but I couldn't think of it. I was blind to any other way of life until the pandemic shut down the world, cutting off my sight to the gym so I could see there was another way.

My husband, David, and I began walking every day as part of our workouts. Adapting was vital for us to continuing thriving. It helped replace some of our time in the gym.

David served in the military, so he was accustomed to walking and running outside, but I had gotten out of the practice. In my earlier years prior to the gym, I jogged, but I had stopped. I even participated in a few marathons. Then I hung up my sneakers for rollerblades. I would faithfully rollerblade about two to three times a week, only in the summer. It was an alternative to doing cardio in the gym. There was a group of us who would meet up to rollerblade. My time outside during this period was purely focused on working out. I enjoyed the rush of whizzing through the trails on my blades, the challenge of making it up hills, and the thrill of accomplishment when I would skate for ten to fifteen miles. However, I stopped because a friend in our group passed away. I let my skates get dusty and old. I tossed the blades and just stayed focused on the gym.

My husband was accustomed to running and he is a fast walker, so it turned into a game for me. I would run so he would have to catch up with me. My running outside was limited. I discovered that running on asphalt and concrete was brutal on my knees and ankles. I was close to crawling after I was done. It was detrimental to my health. So I had to stick to walking.

As I started walking, I began to take note of God's creation. It hit me that God created all of this—the trees and the sky. I was in awe of how he had empowered and equipped man to create parks, homes, buildings, and roads. Looking at his creation humbled me. It made me think about how selfish I had been in taking his creation for granted. I had been jumping into my car, driving to a destination, and missing the sights. I was too focused on getting to my destination, not paying attention to what I was driving past. My eyes were on the road, looking straight ahead.

As I progressed in my walking, I realized this was my opportunity to deepen my relationship with God. This was my time with God—my time to listen and talk to Him. God was extending his hand to me, inviting me to talk with him and to be with him.

I leaned into my walks with vigor. I saw this as my time to learn and grow. Each day, I asked God for three things. First: to see the world and people as he sees them. Second: that his will be done in me as he sees fit, letting this creation of dirt be used for his purpose and will. Third: that the words I speak for his glory would reflect him dwelling in my heart.

I surrendered all of myself to God. I wanted him to show me the way for each day. My life is all about him. My life is not about me but about pleasing and glorifying him. My mission is to please him, to join him in the work he is doing, and to serve him. As I walk, I see God everywhere.

H. S. JACKSON

SEE THE HIDDEN TREASURE

One day as I was walking, I wound up at a ballpark not far from my home. I saw a few cars driving down, but there was not a game for the day. This sparked my interest. It made me wonder what I was missing. I enticed my husband to walk with me to this ballpark. The whole time, he was complaining, stating that there was nothing to see inside the park. We would find nothing but softball diamonds. I did not let his complaining stop me. I kept on going. We walked past the softball diamonds, and I found my hidden treasure—a treasure I had been missing for almost a year. I found a 3.6-mile cross country trail. The trail was unpaved dirt and gravel. I returned to running.

I have fallen in love with this trail that has become my haven. It is the place where I feel closest to God. I know that God brought me to this place so I could have my quiet space to be with him. It is my place where I can open my mind to hear what he has to tell me and where he can give me my assignments for the days, weeks, or months to come. It is the place where I know I will find him at every step and turn I take. It is my place of refuge from the world so I can get in tune with my Father who loves me and who has work for me to do.

My focus is on God as I talk and listen to him. I thank him for my life, health, and family. I thank him for sacrificing his Son so I may have everlasting life. There are times that I do not talk. I am quiet so I can open my mind to listening. Listening means to learn, gain insight, be teachable, be engaged, and nurture a relationship. To listen is to communicate and connect. If I am always talking, I will miss out on what he wants me to see and know. I will miss hearing what it is that he wants me to do. I will miss my assignment.

I will hinder myself in developing a relationship with my Father. It is during my walks on my hidden treasure pathway that I get clarity on my vision and purpose.

My time with God is vital to my mental and physical health. I have found that I cannot be rigid; I must be flexible so I protect the time I have with him. I may not always get to walk at a certain time of the day. What is important is that I get to take my walk or run and that I have time with my Father in my quiet place.

SEE AS GOD SEES

In the summer of 2020, David and I decided to get a dog. As a child, my family had dogs; however, my father did not treat the dogs well, so I did not entertain having a dog as a pet. I love animals, so when my father mistreated ours, it made me sad and angry that he could not see they only wanted his attention and love. I never understood why my father wanted dogs since he was not kind them. I was so glad when our last dog ran away. I cried and hoped he found a better home.

David had a dog prior to our getting married, but his dog had to be put down when she became ill. My husband spoke often of getting a dog, so I finally agreed. God blessed me with my baby girl, Mercedes, a yellow Labrador Retriever. Mercedes became my running and walking buddy on the trail.

My baby girl and I go for a walk or run every morning. I started her walking and running on the trail when she was four months old. She is full of energy, love, and innocence. She sees everyone with love, kindness, and compassion. She is not fearful of reaching out to people or other dogs. She sees all people and dogs as beautiful and with love.

Over time, we have encountered people on the trail who were full of anger and hatred. But not my baby girl. In her eyes, every person is good, no matter how she is treated. She does not understand that not all people reciprocate her love and joy for the world. I am amazed that people start their day full of anger and hatred.

One morning, we were heading back home and encountered another dog with his owner. Both of our dogs were on leashes. Mercedes always wants to greet others and make new friends. As always, she attempted to approach the other dog and its owner, and I restrained her. She leaped toward the dog, and I pulled her back. The dog barked at her, and not in a friendly way. He did not reciprocate her kindness. He growled at her. I immediately pulled Mercedes closer, trying to hurry past.

As we walked past, the other dog leaped at Mercedes, nipping her on her leg, and I hurried along. I did not notice anything initially, but then she whimpered. I stopped to inspect her leg and found that she had a big gash. I was in a panic. We had two miles to get back home. As we were walking, I called her vet. They informed me they were booked for the day. I moved on to calling other places. Every vet I called was booked for the day. I finally called a twenty-four-hour emergency clinic as a last resort. Of course, they were booked until later in the afternoon, which would be almost eight hours later. I continued to walk home. I felt hopeless.

God said to me, "Call her vet one more time. Give it another try."

I followed his instructions and contacted her vet one more time. The vet said, "We do have availability at 11 a.m. Can you get here?" I said I would be there at 10:30 a.m.

I was not messing around. My baby girl needed medical attention. I was overjoyed. God had made a way. I was thankful I had listened and not been obstinate. I would have missed an opportunity for Mercedes to receive treatment. Many times, we give up too easily, thinking that something is not possible. It is for us to keep trying and believing that there is a way. I chose not to give up, and God made a way.

While we were walking home, my little baby was walking with her head up, not showing any discomfort or pain. We encountered another dog and its owner. Instead of Mercedes shying away, she still wanted to greet the dog after what had just occurred. I was astonished. She leaped at the dog and owner to greet them with love, kindness, and compassion.

We finally arrived home. I washed her and she was just looking at me. The pain was setting in and she began whimpering. She was looking at me, perplexed.

I felt as if she was asking me, "Momma, what just happened? I was only trying to greet and spread love. What are we going to do? How can we help people? Do I become like them?"

I was speechless. I felt like I had failed her. I had failed to protect her from evil and pain.

I did not have a response. I took my little girl to the vet later that morning. She was rushed into surgery and had to get stitches. Her bite was a lot worse than her behavior let on. She continued to show love, courage, and resilience. She taught me a lesson I remember to this day. She had been bitten, but she did not allow the bite to change her. Mankind was not going to change her perspective and outlook on believing in and showing love to others. She would continue to see the best in people. She would continue to show love regardless of how she was treated.

While Mercedes was recovering, I continued to reflect on the lesson from this experience. I was sad and angry over what had happened. My baby girl had been bitten by another dog due to my negligence. The owner expressed no remorse or offered to help. It was all my fault. I had let my baby girl down.

I looked to God for help. I sought him for comfort and guidance.

God said to me, "Mercedes has shown you how I see you and all my children. I love you unconditionally. You can do wrong, but know that I am always here. You can keep doing wrong, but know that I forgive you, my love. You can turn your back on me, but I will never turn my back on you. This is how I want you to be. People will cause you pain, heartache, and sadness. Instead of returning the same, I want you to give them love. Love them as I love you, regardless of what they do or say."

I cried and thanked God for this lesson. God used Mercedes to show me how he sees us. He used her to change my perspective of people and my outlook on life. Because of Mercedes I now look to show love, kindness, and compassion regardless of how I am treated. Treat people as if all are beautiful and loved. Turn the other cheek.

In Matthew 18:21-22, Peter asked Jesus, "Lord, how many times shall I forgive my brother or sister who sins against me? Up to seven times?"

Jesus responded, "I tell you, not seven times but seventy-seven times."

Who am I not to love and forgive? If God can, why can't I?

Each day is a new day for me. I begin the day in my quiet place, which prepares me to embrace each day with love, compassion, and forgiveness. There are some days I fall short. I repent and ask God's forgiveness; I ask for him to not give up on me. I am a work in progress. There are other days where I know I let my light shine instead of allowing the darkness to lead. On those days, I give my Father thanks for believing in me. On those days, I am grateful and humbled by my Father.

It is because of my Father that I see people not with my physical eyes but with my spirit. I see their hurt and pain. Nothing they do is personal toward me. They have allowed their negative emotions to create an inner darkness that overshadows the light of the Spirit. Darkness controls their lives, blocking their ability to see beyond their physical sight. I pray they will find their quiet place where they can find and develop a relationship with God, and I pray that you find or have a quiet place—that place that allows you to see beyond the natural world.

Chapter 9
SEE THE TRANSITION

The only thing a person can ever really do is keep moving forward. Take that big leap forward without hesitation, without once looking back. Simply forget the past and forge toward the future.

– ALYSON NOEL, EVERMORE

In life, you will often encounter moments when a door swings open before you. When that door opens, it invites you to take a leap. A leap into the unknown requires a decision, one that only you can make: the decision to either cross the threshold or remain where you are. Staying behind means succumbing to fear. Allowing fear to dictate your path stifles progression.

In his letter to the Corinthians, the Apostle Paul speaks of seizing opportunities. He writes, "But I will stay on at Ephesus until Pentecost, because a great door for effective work has opened to me, and there are many who oppose me" (1 Corinthians 16:8–9). He understands the significance of the open door, recognizing it as a chance for impactful change and growth.

Paul's example teaches us to move beyond complacency and mediocrity, striving for greatness. He didn't let opposition or fear deter him from walking through that open door. Instead, he pressed forward with faith and hope, trusting in his own abilities and the support of a higher power.

Similarly, you are called to press through your fears and doubts and embrace the opportunities before you. The door is open. The invitation is extended. It's up to you to step into your destiny. Beyond the door lies the potential for greatness. You must believe in yourself and in God. He is accompanying you on the journey. Step through the open door with confidence, knowing that you are not alone. God has paved the way for you. What awaits on the other side is intended for you to claim.

Do not allow fear or uncertainty to hold you back. Like Paul, you must seize the moment with courage and determination. The challenges that accompany these opportunities should not deter you but spur you onward. There are decisions to make. Don't hesitate, for opportunities have a way of slipping away if left unattended. Trust in the journey. Step boldly through the open door toward a future filled with promise and purpose.

The time had come for me to move. The quiet time during the pandemic had given me space to pause and reflect. The Spirit inspired me to hunger for more. For nineteen years, I had been undergoing training. I was now equipped and empowered. It was time for me to move on. There was more in me. More was required of me. I was not giving back to God all that he had created within me. It was time to face the "why" of my creation, and I was scared.

Moving on to another season of life is scary. You cannot physically see what is ahead. To move requires trust and faith. Think of Bartimaeus in Mark 10:46–52: he called out to Jesus to heal him. Jesus called him over, but Bartimaeus could not see to get to Jesus. He got to Jesus by following the sound of Jesus' voice. Bartimaeus did not allow his blindness to hinder him from taking the leap to move forward. He jumped up, threw off his coat, and went to Jesus. No one led him by the hand. He found his way on his own following Jesus' voice and spirit. He had faith.

Just as Bartimaeus moved without sight, I had to move without being able to physically see what was to come. I had to take the leap based on faith and hope, seeing with the Spirit and believing in the vision. I had to give up being comfortable and complacent. It was time to move from just existing to living. I had to find my way.

SEE TO MOVE

In Genesis 19, God sent two angels to the cities of Sodom and Gomorrah to destroy the land and people. Sin had taken control of the people. However, the angels sought to save a righteous man named Lot and his family. The two angels instructed Lot and his family to flee.

They said, "Flee for your lives! Don't look back, and don't stop anywhere in the plain! Flee to the mountains or you will be swept away!"

The angels were giving Lot and his family an opportunity for another way, allowing them to move on, but Lot's wife could not move on. She could not leave the past behind. She could not leave that which she had become accustomed to. She wanted to cling to it. She looked back and was turned into a pillar of salt.

In life, you must be willing to move forward, leaving behind that which you have grown accustomed to when it is not for you. Sodom and Gomorrah were towns where sin and evil had won the battle. The people had forsaken morals and values in exchange for selfishness and immorality.

Lot's wife serves as an example of what occurs when you cannot leave the past behind. You miss out on the future. Instead, you must look forward to receiving something greater. Looking forward leads to living out your purpose and realizing your vision. It was time for me to shed my comfortable environment for an environment that would cause me to stretch and grow. I had to step out in faith.

Follow the Vision

The story of Francis Ngannou is an empowering one. Francis is a French Cameroonian mixed martial artist. He currently competes in the heavyweight division for Mixed Martial Arts (MMA) and is a reigning MMA Heavyweight Champion.

His story vividly illustrates how one moves forward, pressing on against the odds. Francis traveled from Cameroon to France, searching for a better life.[6] Turning back was not an option for him. He was inspired to become a boxer by watching the American boxer, Mike Tyson. Watching Mike, he immediately believed that he too could be a champion fighter. Francis' eyes were opened. He saw

---

6   MMA Documentaries, "FRANCIS NGANNOU – THE MOVIE (Documentary)," YouTube, April 26, 2023, video, 55:24, https://youtu.be/cv2xSrzaHKo?si=Baa3Nxdk0lShUr0U.

the vision, believed in his vision, and spoke his vision into reality.

He left his homeland to begin fighting in his late twenties, working tenaciously to become an MAA champion. But when he reached France, Francis was poor, homeless, and hungry. He was forced to scavenge for food out of garbage cans. He lived in a forest and hid from police to avoid being deported back to Cameroon. Ultimately, he was caught by the police and served a few months in prison. However, these hardships did not deter him from his vision. Working hard and being determined were not new concepts to Francis who became a sand miner at the age of at ten years old. He had a vision to become more, which motivated him to claim his purpose and value.

Motivators are the fuel to our action—the fuel to get through the adversity to get to the other side. Motivators will help you get from where you are to where you want to be. You must become aware of your motivators to eliminate the gap between now and the future.

Francis took control of his life using the power of his motivators, which provided him with the strength and courage to put his vision into existence. He believed and made it happen. Francis was the author of his own story.

Francis won his first professional fight, then he continued to move up in the fighting circuit. By the time he lost his first attempt to become an MMA national champion, he already had won the battle. The distance between where he had come from and where he was now was evidence enough of being a winner. A title does not make an individual a winner. What is within a person determines if they are a winner. Francis was no longer a pauper, striving toward his dream to become a fighter. Now, he *was* recognized and respected as an MMA fighter. His was committed and determined to make the unseen visible.

Francis' story illustrates the power of seeing and believing in what you have seen with the Spirit. He was courageous and consistent, and he persevered. He followed through on his priorities, his purpose, and his vision. He was bold and confident, and he believed in the future he saw. Francis had faith.

Francis not only eventually became the MMA champion, but he also paid it forward. He founded a nonprofit organization that provides young boys the opportunity to pursue their dreams in a safe space and learn about sportsmanship. Francis sought to help others believe in making the invisible visible.

My story does not compare with Francis, but we are similar. Just like Francis, I had a vision. My daily text messages I mentioned earlier in the book had grown. I graduated from weekly messages to publishing three books and writing a weekly blog and newsletter. My audience had grown to where I could no longer send out text messages via my phone; I now needed a messaging service.

God was using me through my writing to inspire and motivate others. He showed me that writing is my talent—a talent that inspires and motivates others to see beyond the physical. And I was only just beginning. There was much more work for me ahead.

God was with me. He had equipped me with all I needed. He provided at each step along the way. I just needed to believe and keep pressing onward, taking the leap into the next season of my life and embracing the unknown and uncertain.

ONE MORE THING

One day, I had lunch with one of my mentors, and she told me

God had an assignment for me before I could close the door on this season of my life. I knew one of the assignments, but the other I was not prepared for. There were people I needed to help before I could leave. God revealed to me one individual who was a team member, and another who was an adversary.

During this time, I focused and mediated on my assignment. I spent time daily meditating on this scripture: "You were taught, with regard to your former way of life, to put off your old self, which is being corrupted by deceitful desires; to be made new in the attitude of your minds; and to put on the new self, created to be like God in true righteousness and holiness" (Ephesians 4:22–24). I reflected on its meaning for me. How could I apply it to my life?

I came to realize I needed to shed the emotions and desires that were hindering me and distorting my ability to see. I felt abandoned because team members had been reassigned from my group to another group. I felt anger towards my supervisor for undermining my authority and excluding me from the major decisions that impacted my department. Slowly, my department was being dismantled before my eyes. However, I had to understand that it was not people who were in control, but God. God was using my supervisor to make me uncomfortable so that I would have to move. If things continued peacefully, I would have continued to linger. I had let go of the remnants of my past and put everything to rest.

American poet Walt Whitman wrote a collection of poems, *Leaves of the Grass*, which advocates for embracing life's challenges and opportunities with vigor. Whitman's poetry encourages us to celebrate the adversity of the human experience, to honor individuality, and to confront life's complexities with both courage and authenticity. His work evinces the urgent need to live life fully and with passion, not getting bogged down with regrets and indecision.

Whitman's view encourages us to celebrate the human spirit and move boldly into the unknown. His philosophy inspires me to release my security blanket and press forward. Safety and security are deficiency-based motivators rooted in a perception of lacking. This mindset traps us into a cycle of avoidance and indecision, causing stagnation and comfortability. This can lead us to lose sight of the power of choice—the choice about what is best for our lives. We must believe we can achieve better by trusting in our provider. God promised us hope and a future with prosperity. We believe in this promise, being anchored to him and not to the things of this world, which are provided by him. Overcome inertia by trusting in inner strength and divine guidance. Moving forward releases faith to believe in the greatness within. Take the leap to higher levels of true wellness, trusting in the power and strength that is beyond the self.

I had to trust in him and undertake the assignment that would bring me to the next level. There was a new me and a new world in which I could forge my path. There was no blueprint. I had to step out without being able to see, and I was scared. I listened to others who had second thoughts, and I wanted to join them. My inner voice was wreaking havoc on my positivity as I questioned the feasibility of my business.

I had to get out of my own way, shed my baggage, and believe in who I was and that which was within me. I knew I was somebody who could help and partner with others. There were people I could support. I needed to trust in my Father and follow him. It was time for me. I had been trained, molded, and equipped. I had to move forward to the next phase of my life in trust and faith.

The year before my retirement was vital to the birth of my

business. I looked from the person I was to who I was becoming. I was overwhelmed with praise and thankfulness to God. I had helped my team members; now the time had come for me to help myself. I was my adversary. I had to shed my old self and put on my new self.

God is the source and creator of all. Just as it says in Ephesians 2:10, "For we are God's handiwork, created in Christ Jesus to do good works, which God prepared in advance for us to do." So it is him that I seek to please and glorify, not man. Glorifying God results in living a life that is fulfilling and meaningful. It is by glorifying him that you find peace and wholeness. This wholeness is the evidence of leaning into faith and having hope in the Spirit.

I had to lean into my faith and take action. I was dedicated and committed. Daily, I would read, write, and connect. I needed to develop alliances, partnerships, and connections. We need other people with us to make a vision work. One person is not enough. I had a vision: continue in my writing, coaching, speaking, and training. I had become a certified coach and trainer as a John Maxwell team member. It was now time for me to produce. I would continue my passion of writing and publish another book. I am passionate about serving and helping others. I want them to see as I see, for seeing is instrumental to progressing.

SHED THE BAGGAGE

To see with new eyes, I had to let go of the past that held me back and blocked my sight. I had to leave behind past mistakes, pain, and regrets. None of these spur on forward movement. Holding onto the past blocks vision and purpose. You will waste time floundering, missing out on opportunities that would allow you to advance.

I have a client who I assist in mentoring young men and women in public speaking. These mentees have undergone some trials in their youth. Some have been incarcerated one or more times. The women had childhoods that were not ideal, having experienced abuse or abandonment by one parent or both. Not all of them had troubled backgrounds, but some had made choices that launched them on the wrong path. Some had good parents but followed the crowd and the streets.

My client was offering these young men and women a chance to see more and to embrace a better life. They had another chance. They were being equipped with skills to get back into society and be productive.

They were all motivated to do better, but the majority were not willing to put in the work or effort. Furthermore, their community held them back from doing and becoming better. Their community influenced them greatly. The individuals could see possibilities before them; however, they saw hardships as obstacles that could not be overcome. They were stuck in survival mode. This experience helped me see that these young people were hurting and had built layers of barricades around themselves. I incorporated their insights into my curriculum.

My eyes were opened not just to their situation, but also to my own. I struggled to move forward because the future was full of unknowns, just as they saw their hardships as unpassable. I saw myself huddled in a corner, stymied by new opportunities and needing to change.

I had been in my job for twenty years. I had spent the first seventeen years not seeing and not understanding because I was busy looking at only what was visible. I could get no traction. I now have traction because I am learning to see how God sees.

God is showing me who I am, and I am still evolving. I believe that evolution is a process that never stops. Growing in him will never cease, thus I will continue to develop.

In John 8, Jesus said, "I know where I came from and where I'm going. But you don't know where I come from or where I'm going." What I do know about myself is where I came from. I am following God to find where I am to go. He knows the way. I know I have a purpose and a cause. I am passionate about speaking, training, and writing. When I write, something magical happens within me. I lose track of time. I am enthralled by making my words into a spark of light for another person. I am filled with joy. I am committed to walking in my purpose. I want to help others see as I am learning to see, not with their physical eyes but with the Spirit, making the invisible visible.

There are so many individuals who are lost, floundering through life because they have not uncovered and tapped into their natural talents and gifts. Many individuals have settled for surviving instead of thriving because they have limited vision.

In the Bible, the Pharisees were lost. They followed old doctrine; they failed to see, blinded by their own biases and old ways of thinking, and they were not willing to embrace a new way. Their biased perspectives clouded their vision. Because of their lack of sight, they were their own obstacles, and they sought to hinder others. Jesus refused to allow them to change his way of thinking. He could not be deterred. He was sure of who he was. He was of the Father. The Father had sent him into the world for a purpose. Jesus was in the world to provide salvation and redemption. There was no stopping him.

In comparison, the Pharisees lacked direction and purpose. They were holding onto a way of life that had become extinct. They wanted to remain loyal to the old doctrine. They refused to see. I could not be like the Pharisees. If I followed the way of the Pharisees, I would become stuck and stagnant, and I would remain angry and hostile. I would drift through life blaming others because I had not pursued the purpose of my creation.

God showed me who I was and where I was to go. I was not going to be a ship that failed to use the power of its sails, or a drifter, having no purpose or focus in my life. I would not settle for whatever life gave me. I am a person who knows their purpose and lives in their purpose. I do not allow others or life to control my mindset because I know who I am. I have a cause that I am dedicated to pursuing and executing. I am a servant. I thrive on helping others grow and develop, championing them to be their best so that they, in turn, can bring out the best in others.

Jesus allowed nothing to take him off his course. I will do the same and remain steadfast. I know who I am. As to where I am going, I leave that up to the Father. He is in control and knows the way. It is for me to follow him, and I am following.

Seeing the Wrong Way

It was time for action. God was telling me to press forward. I had reached a fork in the road where I had the choice between two directions, and I did not know which to take. I took a plan of action, believing it was the way to go.

I visited an establishment to execute the next step in my plan. As I was sitting in the reception area, God said, "Get up and get out."

I thought, "No, that is not God. I am on the right path. This action will keep me pressing forward."

Again, the voice said, "Leave." The voice almost made me jump up out of my seat. However, I stayed firmly planted and continued to sit and wait, completing my transaction at the establishment.

On my drive home, I called my husband. I was hesitant to admit to him that I was having second thoughts. But in my spirit, I had a sense of unease. My instincts said there would be repercussions that would block my progress. So, I told my husband what I heard from God, to which he responded that I should have listened. I had essentially wasted my time because that was not the direction God had for me. But I needed more convincing.

Since it was Friday, I decided that before taking action, I would spend time over the weekend to be quiet, listening to God, and asking him what to do. He knows the way.

As I was driving home, I asked God to speak to me. "Please, God, tell me what to do," I said. "Let me see what you see."

I was traveling down a four-lane road, with two northbound and two southbound lanes. I was traveling south, and two cars were headed in my direction traveling north. One of the cars had crossed into my lane, speeding directly towards me. It would not move over. It was not budging. We were going to collide head-on. I thought about God and immediately swerved into the next lane to avoid the crash. The car, for an instant, moved with me, then decided to remain in the first lane. It drove past me, just missing me while still proceeding the wrong way. I was shaken.

I said, "Oh my God, thank you, Jesus."

I pulled over to steady my nerves and looked in my rearview mirror. The car continued to move. It did not stop or slow down.

God said, "Since you have such a hard head, I had to hit you over the head and then splash cold water in your face. I spoke to you in the establishment when you were waiting. I told you to get up. You would not listen. I have your attention now, don't I?"

I said, "Absolutely."

I heard God loud and clear: "Wrong way."

I was headed in a direction that he had not planned. He let me see. I was to follow him. I was being obstinate and disobedient to what he wanted me to do.

God sees when I cannot see. My understanding is flawed and clouded by my selfishness. I do not have clarity and understanding; however, God does. I must depend on God to accomplish what I am unable to see. Imagine if Peter had not taken one more look when Jesus told him to cast his net into the water again. Imagine if he had not followed Jesus' direction. He would have missed out on being a disciple and living his purpose. After his encounter with Jesus, he stopped being a fisherman of fish and became a fisherman of men. One must stop looking at what can only be seen with the physical eye and look to see through God's eyes instead.

One must move, not knowing what the future will be. What you know is that you have faith and hope to believe in what cannot be seen. You have faith and hope that you will have a future. There is a plan you cannot see; however, you believe. Use the power of the Spirit's sight to move you forward and follow your passion—a passion that takes you through the roadblocks you encounter. Roadblocks and obstacles are part of the process. Believe and follow.

Remaining restless and confined is not an option. Staying will not result in fulfillment and achievement. I am compelled to follow the sight of the Spirit; I have faith and hope in my future.

Renewed in these convictions, I was excited and apprehensive about the journey. However, I was committed to enjoying whatever God had for me, embracing and looking forward to each day's potential and uncertainties. I needed to believe in the sight of the Spirit. However, there was another barrier in my sight that I had to conquer first.

Chapter 10

EVICT UNBELIEF

Now faith is confidence in what we hope for and assurance about what we do not see.

– Hebrews 11:1

There are five key components in Hebrews 11:1. They are faith, confidence, hope, assurance, and the unseen. When woven together, these five components create a complete picture of what true faith encompasses. Let's analyze each of these components and their application.

The first component, faith, serves as the cornerstone of your spiritual journey. It's not merely a passive belief but rather an active force that shapes your decisions, actions, and worldview. Faith is the lens through which you interpret experiences and build the foundation for your relationship with God. You get to actively participate in the gifts and choices God gives you.

Confidence, the second component, is a deep-seated trust in God's character and promises—not in human achievement. This confidence empowers you to stand firm in the face of adversity, knowing your trust is placed in a source that is far greater than you. It is the kind of confidence that enabled David to face Goliath and Daniel to enter the lion's den.

Hope, the next component, goes beyond wishful thinking. Hope means having a confident expectation anchored in God's faithfulness. It is forward-looking but grounded in the history of God's fulfilled promises. This hope and conviction of future glory gives strength so we may persevere through present challenges.

Assurance is the inner conviction that validates our faith. It is the spiritual equivalent of having a title deed to a property: though you may not physically possess it yet, you have legal ownership. This assurance comes from the Holy Spirit as your witness, confirming God's promises in your heart.

The "things not seen" are a reminder that faith operates in the realm beyond physical sight. This doesn't make these realities any less real; rather, it points to a deeper kind of seeing: spiritual discernment. Like Moses, who persevered because he saw "him who is invisible", you are called to look beyond surface appearances to eternal realities (Hebrews 11:27).

These five elements—faith, confidence, hope, assurance, and the unseen—work in harmony create a robust faith for living. This type of faith provides confidence and stability. It provides hope, directing our gaze forward. It gives us assurance, which confirms our path. And acceptance of the unseen opens you up God's supernatural work in your life.

By understanding and embracing these components, your faith

becomes a transformative force in your daily life. It enables you to face challenges with courage, patience, and purpose, knowing your faith is built on the solid ground of God's unchanging character and promises.

True faith encompasses not just believing but confidently hoping and envisioning beyond what can be seen. Faith means trusting in God who sees all and works all things together for our good.

I had to put this scripture into practice. I decided to pursue my purpose and use the talent I had been gifted. This required being all in, taking ownership of myself and giving control to my Father. I needed to take the leap to stand on my faith. In Mark 9:14–29, there was a boy possessed by a demon. His father had approached the disciples, but the disciples had been unable to help. The father was at his wit's end. As he anxiously sought healing for his son, he began to doubt healing was possible. His son had been suffering for quite some time. The father was seeking relief. Jesus was his last resort. His final chance.

The father asked Jesus, "But if you can do anything, take pity on us and help us."

Jesus responded, "If you can? Everything is possible for the one who believes."

The father then cried out, "I do believe, but help me overcome my unbelief!"

Just like this father, I have faith, but I struggle with unbelief in my ability to withstand the storms that come. I am confident and courageous; however, the storms can be overwhelming. I allow the attacks of individuals to plant seeds of doubt in my mind. I know these attacks are part of the process. They are part of getting to the other side, which holds progress and achievement. But sometimes, they are still hard for me to withstand. There are times when the attacks are so powerful I feel I will not be able to achieve the outcome I have set out to accomplish.

Help My Unbelief

In Mark 6:6, Jesus makes an observation. The text says, "He was amazed at their lack of faith." These words encapsulate a profound truth about the human condition: we have an enormous capacity for unbelief and contempt, which hinders us from realizing the full extent of what we can achieve.

In the surrounding passage, Jesus returns to his hometown of Nazareth to teach in the synagogue. However, instead of being met with faith and acceptance, he encounters skepticism and doubt from those who knew him. Despite witnessing his miracles and hearing his teachings, the people of Nazareth fail to believe in him. Their lack of faith astounds Jesus, highlighting the profound impact unbelief can have on a person's life.

Unbelief is a pervasive barrier that prevents you from embracing the possibilities that lie beyond your immediate comprehension. It restricts vision, confines potential, and blinds us to the extraordinary opportunities awaiting. Allowing doubt to cloud judgment limits and stifles the growth that comes from embracing the unknown.

The attacks make me antsy and anxious, but being attacked means that I am doing something right. I am on the right path. Attacks are part of the process I must go through to achieve the vision I have painted. I have faith and trust in the Father. What I do not always have is faith in myself and my own ability to withstand. The Lord keeps his promise. It is my promise to myself that I have difficulty keeping because of the discomfort it brings. But I know that being uncomfortable is how I experience growth and continue evolving.

I have a compelling desire to serve God. There is a driving force within me to join my Father in the work he is doing and change this world for the better. Joining the Father means that I will be attacked. As much as is given, that much will be required. It is required that I suffer and overcome attacks to live and follow my purpose. For over thirty years, I know God has been with me. God sustained in me in my last job for twenty years. There were many times I did not think I would be able to endure, but I did.

I now faced another hurdle. A major storm was brewing. I had to leave my job of twenty years and take the leap to progress. I was terrified.

For twenty years, I had been secure; however, I was not truly secure. I worked in an environment that was toxic. I had to be mindful of every word and action. Individuals were jealous of my position and what I had accomplished. Because of their envy, other employees were quick to file a complaint or allegation; these could result in an investigation, and I often had to defend myself. In my career, I have been attacked on both sides: by subordinates and superiors. I built my armor on God and His Word. This armor had many kinks in it, but because of the armor, I was able to withstand for twenty years.

In those twenty years, I had grown secure. Now, I had to take my security to the next level to become even more secure in my faith.

For twenty years, I had allowed myself to become programmed into working a job I was not sad to leave. I embraced and celebrated leaving. What I did not embrace or celebrate was again being uncomfortable as I took my faith in myself to the next level. I questioned myself. I asked, "Do I have what it takes to keep going?"

I answered my own doubts and reminded myself, "God has made me the promise of hope and a future. I must hold on to this promise to make it a reality. I must put in the work. I must believe in me, making his promise a reality."

In the last thirty years, I had accomplished much. I took that as evidence, clearly showing what I could accomplish in the future. The time had come for me to do more. I had to go deeper into myself to get to the next level in my life. The time had come for me to put up or shut up. In Deuteronomy 1:6, God says, "You have stayed long enough at this mountain." There is a time to stay, and there is a time to move. You must know when to move. The time had come for me to leave the mountain.

Jeff Henderson, motivational speaker, author, and pastor, says, "It never gets easy, but it becomes less difficult if you will keep moving forward."[7] In other words, just take a step; it will get easier to keep taking steps once you start moving. I had become accustomed to the mountain that was my job. A job where I was miserable, unaccepted, and unappreciated. In meetings, I was typically in the minority, surrounded by white males who did not want me in the meeting. I worked a stressful job in which senior leaders constantly scrutinized my work and found excuses to attack my performance.

I have concluded that no person should remain where they are if they are unwanted. God will make the mountain uncomfortable, forcing you to act. Staying on the job for twenty years made it difficult for me to move. In my reflections, I realized that prior to working with this agency, I had moved around to a new job every five years. After that, I became complacent, settling. I had gotten

---

7   Jeff Henderson, "The Scary First Step," *FOR*, December 13, 2022, https://mailchi.mp/bf71ad8e491c/todaystheday-8015071?e=b6c94ed791.

stuck at the mountain. I could not get stuck at the mountain. The time had come to be courageous—to embrace moving up to higher levels of living and growth.

God tells the Israelites it is time to move so that they may receive his promise. Staying at the mountain would have caused them to miss out on the opportunities and advancement God planned for them: a new land of abundant resources, where the people could expand their wings and tap into their potential.

This what God wants us to do. Movement requires being uncomfortable, embracing what is new, and shedding the known for the unknown. It requires believing in self and in him, having confidence in your skills and capabilities. We must have hope in the future, seeing not with physical sight but with the Spirit. It is faith not in the "*no*" but in the *knowing*—knowing that you will reach what you are striving to achieve.

Staying where you are limits potential. That potential, when unleashed, results in higher levels of achievement and growth. When we realize this potential, we drown out the voices of doubt, fear, and limiting beliefs with voices of hope, strength, and belief.

This chapter has been the hardest for me to write because I had to dig within me to reveal my vulnerability and expose my weakness. My weakness is me. I must get out of my way, or I will hinder my progression in realizing God's promise.

As I reflect on my life for the past thirty years, the evidence is clear that God has been my protector. I received my master's degree while working part-time. And while working part-time, I was able to afford a car and an apartment. I did not lack for anything. After graduating with my master's, I wandered for ten years, having three to four different jobs. I did not remain at any one job for more than five years. Each time I lost a job, I secured another job. Now, I was facing a new season in my life, and I was terrified because I had to dig deeper within myself. I had to conquer the disbelief that was in me.

Doubt and fear were running rampant, controlling my thoughts and emotions as I exited my job to build a new career. I was battling myself and pleading with God to stop the storm raging within me, but I was the one who had to stop the storm.

My doubts and fears had taken up residence in my mind. And what the mind focuses on is what a person will become. The mind speaks words that either empower or disable.

In Matthew 12:37, the Bible reminds us of the profound significance of our words: "For by your words you will be acquitted, and by your words you will be condemned." Indeed, words are the vessels through which you express thoughts, feelings, and emotions. They are crafted by the intricate interplay of the stomach (emotions), heart (feelings), and brain (thoughts) within us.

As a being endowed with divine capabilities, you wield the power to shape your reality through your words. Just as God spoke the universe into existence, your words have the potential to mold your destiny and influence the outcome of your life. You are entrusted with the gift of communication to bring about good, mirroring the divine intention behind creation.

Yet, with this power comes responsibility. You are called to exercise discernment and love in your speech, forming patterns that empower and inspire yourself as well as others. Your words should reflect sound reasoning and goodwill. They should bear fruit that is abundant and nourishing to yourself and those around you.

Recognize the weight of accountability that accompanies your speech. Use the power of words wisely, speaking words of kindness, encouragement, and truth. Be mindful of the legacy you create with your speech. Your words have the potential to shape not only your own destiny but also the world around you.

After God, I am the person I talk to most in life. As such, it is imperative to monitor my moods and emotions. Both impact the five things I control: my thoughts, feelings, words, beliefs, and actions. The words I spoke to myself during my career transition were working havoc over my life. The conversations I had with myself were causing me to lose conviction in my business—my driving purpose and passion.

One day, I woke up at 5 a.m. I started the day reading the Word. I prayed and then wrote for a short time. Suddenly, panic hit me. My heart began pounding so hard, I thought it was going to come out of my chest. I felt as if the walls in my home were closing in on me.

I said to myself, "Who do I think I am to believe I could keep pressing forward toward having a business?" I was not worthy of being a business owner. I did not have the strength nor the tenacity. My inner gremlin was busy casting doubt and fear.

Thoughts were stampeding in my mind. Next, I said, "I am not going to be able to leave my job. It is not possible. It is not going to happen. I am creating a mess. All that I have envisioned is not going to become a reality."

I felt as if my whole world was crumbling around me. I came to a complete standstill, paralyzed with fear.

I did not know what to do. I looked at the clock; it was now 8:00 a.m. Both of my furry babies were looking at me impatiently, wanting to eat and go for their walk. I had to pull myself together. I called my husband. He attempted to talk me over the mountain of unbelief I had constructed. He asked me, "Where is your faith?"

I responded, "I have faith, but I need help with my unbelief." I needed help. I needed help from God.

I had to get out of the house. I fed my baby girls, and we headed out for our walk. I began talking to God. I asked him to help me see what he sees. I told him that I put my trust in him and that I knew he was in control—that whatever happened was what he had purposed and planned. I needed to follow him and believe, but I was failing him. I was lacking. I was allowing the world to win in my thinking. For the remainder of the day, I stayed focused on God and his Word. I clung to his presence, to see, think, and feel as he does. I knew I had to see with the faith he had in me.

God gave me power to press forward in my purpose. In turn, I had given that power over to fear. I was fearful because there was no roadmap. After being comfortable for twenty years, I was on a new path, and I had only one option: to take the next step. The only option was to get out of the boat and walk on the water—to take Jesus' hand and believe, unlike Peter, who allowed the rough waters frighten him and stop him from walking. I needed to keep walking. I had spent too much time distracted and distressed from overthinking my abilities. Now, I wanted God to rebuke the storm I created, but I had to rebuke the storm for myself. It was a storm of my own creation that I needed to cease.

OVERTHINKING

For ten days, my mind stayed in overdrive, thinking I would not succeed. My negative inner voice was shouting at me to stop, give up, go lay down on the couch, pull the covers over my head, and let life pass me by. This overthinking fueling my unbelief in myself.

The price for overthinking is high. The price is nonrefundable and yields no reward. Overthinking caused me to flounder around, being unfocused and working at fifty percent, wasting time that should have been spent on business projects. I wanted to turn back. I painted a picture of tragedy. I was going to be an utter and complete failure in my business. I wanted to go back. I was stuck looking behind me.

I was like Lot and his wife in Sodom and Gomorrah. Lot and his family were living in a city where the people had no boundaries. God sent angels to the city to witness just how bad the city had become. The angels found the city deplorable. It had to be destroyed. The people were not salvageable. The angels found that Lot, his wife, and his children were the only remaining righteous people in the entire city. They saved Lot and his family by escorting them out of the city to safety and instructing them to flee to the mountains. However, Lot begged to go to a nearby city. He felt a city was safer than relying on the mountain God had selected.

Lot gave a city more trust than he gave God. This is what I was doing: giving my job more trust and power than I gave to God.

The angels agreed to Lot's request but told him and his wife to flee and not look back. Lot's wife could not follow instructions. She was disobedient and looked back, which caused her to be turned into a pillar of salt. She could not let go of the world to follow God.

Similarly, I was finding it hard to let go of my job, but I needed to move forward. I was not going to get to the next level in my life holding onto a job. I knew and believed God has so much in store for me that could not be realized if I did not let go. I had to let go to go up. I had to see with faith and obedience and follow Him. I had to put a lid on my overthinking, closing off the negative thoughts that hindered and blocked me from taking the next step. I had to stop looking back. I had to move forward to embrace the next season of my life.

There was no going back. I had made too much progress in my business to give up. I had written three books, developed my skills as a speaker and trainer, created and launched product lines, and formed alliances. I was making all the moves to keep pressing forward. However, I still lacked faith in myself.

I was drawing conclusions that the future was out of my hands when I actually needed to control the five things I had in my power. I had to stop the negative overthinking, which only created situations of gloom and doom. I had to stop drawing conclusions that were not grounded in facts. God had been covering and protecting me for all my life. He had been molding and training me. It was now time to deliver on what he had developed in me.

In his bestselling book, *Soundtracks: The Surprising Solution to Overthinking,* Jon Acuff says to ask yourself these three questions when overthinking:

1. Is it true? Look at the facts to determine if the thought is true or false.

2. Is it kind? The thought must be uplifting, or it will not do you any good.

3. Is it helpful? The thought must aid you in moving forward, not going backwards or standing still.[8]

I have added three additional questions to this framework as

---

[8] Jon Acuff, *Soundtracks: The Surprising Solution to Overthinking* (Baker Books, 2021).

I've used it in my life:

1. Does it add value to my passion and purpose? Thinking negative thoughts will detract from your cause. They will cause you to waste time and energy that you could be spending on actions to make the unseen visible.

2. Who and what does it impact? The conclusions you form in your mind affect you, those around you, and how you treat them. For example, what I do impacts my husband, affecting his attitude and behavior, and so on.

3. How does it help me progress? I have found that when I overthink, I only waste time and energy, make false assumptions, and procrastinate. None of these help me move forward.

Overthinking was feeding my fear and giving me nothing in return. I had to learn to see past it.

See Past Fear

Fear is a strange thing. It can mean Forget Everything and Run, or Face Everything and Rise. It is my choice.

Choosing the latter does not come naturally, as we see throughout the Bible. Moses didn't want to lead his people out of Egypt. He didn't want to speak to crowds either. But God persisted and insisted. Moses was to lead his people. God became impatient with his excuses. Moses had only one choice: to answer the call. God knew what he had created Moses for.

Jeremiah 1:4 whispers to our souls, "Before I formed you in the womb I knew you." This verse serves as a reminder of your intrinsic gifts. These natural gifts—the innate abilities you possess from birth—are not random occurrences but deliberate endowments designed to assist you throughout the journey of your life.

Each person is uniquely equipped with the tools necessary to undertake and fulfill their purpose. It is incumbent upon you to unearth these gifts. Recognize and nurture them. Utilize them not to dismantle but to construct—not to tear down but to build up the world around you.

Utilizing these gifts necessitates a profound awareness: an awareness of self, grounded in the unwavering belief in one's capabilities. This knowing transcends mere recognition. It encompasses a deep-seated clarity that one's identity is not defined by external influences but by personal truths. These truths serve as the bedrock upon which your confidence and self-efficacy thrive, empowering you to dictate your own narrative and wield authority over your destiny.

With knowing comes faith and hope: faith in the efficacy of your abilities and hope as you realize your aspirations. It is this triumvirate of knowing, faith, and hope that propels you forward on your journey of self-discovery and purpose.

God knew me. God created me for my destiny and makes no mistakes. I had to trust him to train my mind to see beyond fear. Fear is a distraction that can control the mind and thoughts. Fear is an assassin of faith, and hope is the killer of the assassin.

In Matthew 14:22–33, Jesus Christ walks on the water and invites Peter to join him. As Peter is walking on the water, he moves his focus from Jesus to the storm and the waves, which causes him to sink. He cries out to Jesus for help. Jesus states, "You of little faith, why did you doubt?" Doubt is the product of fear. Combat fear with hope. Hope is the fuel that moves you to take action. Have faith in what the Spirt knows and sees, which empowers you to execute and produce. When you get out of the boat, do not succumb to fear. Instead, cast your anchor on hope.

Hope inspires movement while fear causes paralysis, preventing you from taking the actions required for progression, growth, and evolution. You cannot allow fear to become rooted in your mind. Fight for what you want, believe in what could be possible, and know that the unseen can become seen.

I have come to realize two things. First and foremost, God is my source. He will provide me with what I need. Second, I had to use the power of my mind. My thoughts are my power. Thoughts must be monitored and controlled.

Thoughts impact the ability to move forward. They can become strongholds that block progression, becoming a hindrance. Thoughts can create illusions of safety and security, cause you to doubt your capabilities, trick you into remaining in situations that are not to your benefit, or lead you to become complacent. To progress, you need to break the stronghold of your thoughts, changing your way of thinking. If you fail to change your thoughts, which dictate your responses to circumstances, you may block your progression. You will remain stuck on a wheel, running like a caged mouse, and providing entertainment to others. A mouse on a wheel expends energy but does not make any progress traveling to a destination. The wheel just turns in a circle until someone releases the mouse from the wheel. Just as with the mouse, if your thoughts do not change, you will remain stuck on the wheel, not moving forward, making no progress. You must change your thoughts, or you will remain in the same situation. Your thoughts cage your mind. What you think is what you believe; both are reflected in your actions.

In the movie, *Groundhog Day*, starring Bill Murray, Bill awakens every morning to discover that it is Groundhog Day again. The same day keeps occurring over and over again. He initially thinks replaying the day is to his advantage until he learns that he may spend an eternity in the same place, seeing the same people every day without end.

He had to change his thoughts and actions; he was selfish, uncaring about others and their needs. He had to change his way of thinking and understand that life was about being of service to others. Bill had to learn to care for others to get out of the cycle of Groundhog Days, thereby breaking the stronghold of selfish thoughts and practices.

The same principle applies to each of us. You remain stuck in the same cycle until you change your thoughts. Do not be a conformer to this world, but be committed to renewal and transformation.

Recall Esau, Jacob's son. For a bowl of soup, Esau relinquished his heritage to his brother, Jacob. Esau had no appreciation or regard for his inheritance. His stomach was more important than fulfilling the purpose for which he was created. Fast forward: he sought to claim his inheritance later, but it was too late. His mind had not truly changed; he only sought what he thought was his right to claim, and he sought this right for selfish reasons. I had to change my way of thinking to receive the blessings God planned for my life.

As it says in Ephesians 4:23–24, we must seek "to be made new in the attitudes of your minds; and to put on the new self, created to be like God in true righteousness and holiness." I had to let myself be birthed. I had to change my thoughts so I could press forward. I had to break the stronghold of my thoughts. My daily challenge and desire is to let my light remain plugged into the power source. The strength of my light will depend on my foundation in the source.

In times of trials and hardships, darkness will appear. But the scriptures say Jesus came into the world to give us life and light: "In him was life, and that light was the light of all mankind. The light shines in the darkness, and the darkness has not overcome it" (John 1:4–5). Later, Jesus reemphasized this theme when he tells the crowd,, "I am the light of the world. Whoever follows me will never walk in darkness, but will have the light of life." (John 8:12).

His light will guide your light out of the darkness; just believe, have faith, and do not allow darkness to overtake your light. Remember Job? His world was crashing down. He had lost all that he had—both material and physical health. He had nothing else to live for; however, not once did he give up on the Lord. The Lord was his source, rejuvenated his light, and caused it to beam even brighter. Similarly, your light is extended to the source: the son, Jesus. He will get you through; he is the true light who gives light to everyone.

I needed to believe in my beam. I had to believe in the life that God made possible. I could not allow my light to be extinguished or overshadowed. I needed to stand firm in keeping my light connected to the source to pull me through my darkness.

My foundation to the source was anchored, but I had to work on myself. I had to return to my roots, utilizing the F.A.T. principle: have Faith to Act and Think. I had to use the power of my mind to replace the negative thoughts with positive thoughts. I needed to silence and overpower the pessimistic voice that would sabotage my vision. This required me to put my faith into action and to control my thoughts instead of letting my thinking control me.

There are 365 verses throughout the Bible in which God tells us, "Fear not." Do you think maybe he knows something we do not?

He knows fear will cloud judgment and result in unbelief. My fear was causing me to believe I was trapped and powerless. My eyes did not see faith. I was relying on my strength, not God's. I only allowed my eyes to transmit that which was visible, making me believe that my path forward was closed. Fear caused me to lose focus and faith, closing my mind and closing the door on God.

This is exactly what the world and the enemy seek: to trick me into turning *from* God instead of turning *to* him. The world wants me to fail. Its criticisms are designed to make me believe that there is only one way and that's it. But that is not it—this is only the beginning.

The world had been my training ground for thirty years. There was more to come for me. I was not done. I needed to endure, persevere, and believe. This was my time to be my best self and conquer the world. The world had no hold over me unless I gave it the power and the authority, which I had done by fueling my negative self. I had to take my power and authority back. I had to conquer my unbelief.

In 2 Kings 6, Elisha was guiding to the people of Israel regarding the continuous attacks from the King of Aram. The Lord supernaturally provided Elisha with the king's plans so Elisha could warn the people of Israel. The king became frustrated and angry because, at every turn, his plans were foiled. He believed there was a traitor in his midst. He became furious when he was informed that it was Elisha who was receiving the information from God and passing it along to the people.

The king sought to kill Elisha. He sent a vast army to surround Elisha and his servant. The servant looked outside to see the army and became distraught. He was fearful and asked Elisha what they should do. Surely, their demise was imminent. They were outnumbered and had no way of escaping. Elisha, however, was not afraid or upset.

Elisha's eyes were opened, seeing that there was no need to fear. He knew he was safe. He was working for the Lord, doing God's will, and being obedient. As such, the Lord was with him.

Elisha said to his servant, "Do not be afraid. Those who are with us are more than those who are with them" (2 Kings 6:16). Then Elisha prayed, "Open his eyes, Lord, so that he may see" (2 Kings 6:17). The Lord opened the servant's eyes so that when he looked out, he too saw the hills full of horses and chariots of fire surrounding Elisha—he saw God's army ready at the ready to defend them. The eyes of Elisha's servant had to be opened to see the protection beyond the darkness. His eyes saw beyond his terror.

I must have faith in myself to silence my fears. I am frightened when in the dark; however, I am not in the dark alone. God is with me. "For God has not given us a spirit of fear, but one of power, love, and sound judgment" (2 Timothy 1:7, CSB).

Look at Him. See with clarity the sovereignty and power of the Lord to combat fear. He created me, equipping me with all I need. I must keep my focus on Him. He is in control. What happens is whatever he has predestined and determined.

In Mark 5:25–29, there is a powerful story of a woman who suffered from a debilitating condition for twelve long years. Despite seeking help from numerous physicians and experts, she found no relief and her condition worsened. Amidst her despair, she clung to a glimmer of hope: the belief that Jesus could heal her. She said, "If I just touch his clothes, I'll be made well." Upon touching him, she was instantly healed.

This woman's story is a poignant reminder of the transformative power of personal agency. Despite the odds stacked against her, she refused to relinquish control of her own destiny. With unwavering determination, she pressed through the crowd, knowing that if she could just touch the hem of Jesus' garment, she would find the healing she desperately sought.

The woman was determined and self-disciplined to seize what she wanted. She exemplified the essence of personal power: the ability to take control of one's own life, to defy the limitations imposed by circumstance, and to pursue one's goals with relentless tenacity. She refuses to be defined by her illness or constrained by the opinions of others. Instead, she seized the opportunity to enact change in her life, trusting in her own intuition and inner strength.

This woman's story serves as a powerful reminder that personal power is not bestowed upon us by external forces but rather cultivated from within. It is the culmination of self-awareness, resilience, and the courage to take decisive action in pursuit of our dreams.

Draw inspiration and motivation from this woman with the hemorrhage. Let us harness our own personal power to navigate life's challenges, overcome adversity, and ultimately, manifest our deepest desires. Like her, you possess the innate ability to shape your destiny and create the life you envision.

Here are four essential elements to cultivating personal power:

1. Self-awareness: Take time to reflect on your beliefs, values, and goals. Understand your strengths and weaknesses, and be honest with yourself about areas in which you can improve.

2. Mindset: Cultivate a growth mindset that embraces challenges and sees failures as opportunities for growth. Believe in your ability to learn and adapt in any situation. Replace self-limiting beliefs with empowering thoughts that propel you forward.

3. Self-discipline: Personal power is not just about having

potential; it's about taking consistent action towards your goals. Develop self-discipline by setting clear intentions, creating routines, and holding yourself accountable for your actions.

4. Emotional resilience: Build resilience by learning to manage stress, setbacks, and negative emotions. Practice mindfulness, deep breathing, and other stress-reducing techniques to stay grounded in challenging times. Remember, it's not about avoiding difficulties but about how you respond to them that matters.

Harnessing personal power is transformative in the following ways:

1. Increases confidence: As you tap into your personal power, you'll notice a boost in confidence and self-assurance. You'll trust yourself to make decisions and take bold actions, knowing that you have the inner strength to handle whatever comes your way.

2. Fortifies resilience: Personal power equips you with the resilience to bounce back from setbacks and overcome obstacles. Instead of feeling defeated by challenges, you'll see them as opportunities for growth and transformation.

3. Improves relationships: When you're grounded in your personal power, you'll approach relationships from a place of authenticity and integrity. You'll set healthy boundaries, communicate effectively, and attract people who respect and support your journey.

4. Supports goal attainment: With personal power driving you forward, you'll be unstoppable in pursuing your goals and dreams. Whether it's advancing in your career, starting

a business, or embarking on a personal passion project, you'll have the clarity, focus, and determination to make it happen.

The two weeks before I left my job, I had lost my power and sound judgment. On October 21, 2022, I took back my power.

After twenty years, I left my job—one with which I had grown extremely accustomed to. I went from a six figure job to a small retirement fund. I took the leap to live and choose true wellness. I was striving to live a life that maximixed my potential in all spheres, not just financially. Despite all the reasons to stay, my wellness was more important than the job I held. Each day, I dreaded traveling to a job that left me empty and discontent. The Spirit had me yearning to do more and become more.

In the John Maxwell training program, one of the mentors and coaches was Paul Martinelli. Paul became successful as a coach by stepping out in his faith. Specifically, Paul jumped without a parachute to become a coach. He trusted in the process, knowing he would have a landing. Paul is a successful coach who specializes in mindset and growth. I decided to follow Paul's example. I jumped.

The day after my retirement, I woke up at 5 a.m. on a Saturday morning. I was lying in bed reflecting on my life for the past thirty years. I had jumped from the plane with no parachute. I had to make room for what was to come. I had to give up in order to go up.

I suddenly jumped out of bed. I began walking and shouting throughout my house. I yelled, "Today is the first day of the rest of my life. Fear and grief have no place in my mind or home. They are being evicted today. I will succeed in my business. I am worthy. I have the knowledge and skills. I am powerful. I am beautiful. I am a survivor. I will thrive."

I continued praying and talking for about fifteen minutes. I felt twenty pounds lighter. I was releasing the excess weight I had picked up.

I changed my thinking and words to the present and future tense. I stated, "I am going to succeed. Nothing is impossible with God. I have faith that will move my mountain. I will see with faith and not fear. I am pressing forward."

I was taking the first step in making my career a reality. I decided: I will have faith in me; I will silence the negative emotions and thoughts.

My emotions and moods caused overthinking and impacted the stories I told myself. My stories affected my faith. Now, I was determined that the stories I told must be grounded in God's Word. His Word would feed my faith in myself. I realized that just as I had faith in him, I I needed to have faith in me. Having faith did not mean the road ahead will be easy, but it did mean I would be equipped to handle the obstacles as they came. Faith was the key to unlocking my future. As I went forward with faith, I believed in what cannot be seen. I had hope for my future and my ability to face adversity, increase my capacity, and transform.

To keep myself pressing forward, I decided from now on, I would lean into these five things: what I say, what I believe, what I think, what I feel, and what I do. My faith would serve as my anchor, helping me control my emotions and thoughts as I navigated through life's challenges.

Emotions and thoughts have five outcomes: they shape mindset, which shapes our reality; they support movement toward progress; they impact productivity and efficiency; they feed into attitude, which affects altitude; lastly, they impact the journey of becoming the person I was created to be. By harnessing these five elements and aligning them with my faith, I was ready to strive for clarity, purpose, and resilience. I trusted these attributes would guide my actions and shape my journey towards personal growth and fulfillment.

In this season, I learned that, ultimately, I am in control of my emotions and thoughts. Emotions and thoughts are like water. I heard this analogy and I have applied it to my faith. Let's look at three things that are impacted by boiling water: an egg, a carrot, and coffee.

In boiling water, the egg becomes hardened. The shell remains the same, but inside, the egg solidifies. Emotions and moods can cause you to become hardened to people and the world, impacting how you see and view others. If you're like the egg, you have a negative outlook causing you to stall in your progression to higher levels of achievement and growth.

The carrot in boiling water becomes soft, losing its firmness. Emotions and moods can cause you to cower, lacking courage to pursue your passion, dreams, and vision. You allow what others say to hinder you from believing in what you see. If you are most like the carrot, you doubt what you can do, and instead of moving forward, you bury your hopes and dreams.

Coffee in boiling water does not change. Coffee changes water. The coffee can withstand. It does not allow its environment or elements to be in control. It is in control. Faith must be like coffee. I cannot allow outside elements to change my faith. I must use my faith to change the elements. My faith will take control of my emotions and thoughts, and it will impact my outcomes.

I will place my faith in God. God is the pilot of my plane; with him, I will soar to greater heights. I must give up good to obtain better. I had to silence my unbelief toward being able to achieve better. I am embracing the adventure to seize what is better. I have evicted unbelief, reclaiming my faith in myself.

With God as my pilot, I now enable and empower others to keep pressing forward through their obstacles, trials, and hardships. I strive to help others create their vision, not allowing their environment or others to place a ceiling on what they can accomplish. I was excited yet fearful of my purpose. My vision is to continue publishing books, expanding my training to host an annual empowerment growth experience conference, mentor youth, and help individuals get back on the right path.

I am also the Founder and Executive Director of Ava's Pathways, a nonprofit dedicated to helping women overcome challenges and life transitions that have made them feel stuck. I provide life and wellness coaching to help them meditate, reflect, and regain focus on their own pathway through life. Choosing their pathway incorporating the three B's - Believe, Become and Belong. BELIEVE in authentic identity grounded in fundamental truths rather than societal pressures. This requires using evidence of strengths, values, and purpose to be the guiding compass. BECOME this vision through consistent, intentional actions that gradually align external reality with internal convictions until existence naturally expresses core identity. BELONG to a community that celebrates the authentic journey. A community that provides both the challenge and support necessary for sustainable transformation while reinforcing beliefs and accelerating becoming. We focus on how they can nurture and recenter themselves. As they do, they experience a greater dependence on the Spirit than on the physical sight that has limited them. I have felt more purposeful than ever while working with these women.

God gave me the freedom to pursue my purpose. I now had to make decisions to keep me pressing forward in this purpose. I turned to Philippians 1:6. This scripture serves as my anchor, giving me confidence that there is a good work in me. There is a purpose that I must carry out to completion. I needed to have the faith to press on and see myself as God sees me. I became more confident and steadfast, and I strengthened my belief in making the unseen visible. I was committed to leaning on the Spirit to see and be my guide.

Chapter 11

SEE YOURSELF

Whether you think you can or think you can't, you're right.

– HENRY FORD

What you see is compelling and will encourage you to achieve what you desire. But you must look deep within yourself to discover what potential you can contain.

Haseena was not the name I was given at birth. When my parents converted to Islam when I was four years old, they adopted the Islamic tradition of taking on a new Arabic name. The choosing of a name is important in the Islamic faith because it represents who you are; it represents leaving behind what has defined you and embracing a new birth of yourself. My mom looked through an Arabic name book and chose "Haseena." The Arabic meaning of Haseena is "beautiful," and Shaheed means "a great warrior." God directed my mother to choose my name. It was given to me that I might see myself and believe. Believing is fuel for our life's journey.

I invite you to learn what your own name means and meditate on it. Each name, whatever its origin, has a history and significance that reflects your value. What you meditate upon is what you will expand upon. Let your own name be an affirmation of your beauty, strength, and authority. Affirmations equip you and lay the foundation for how you handle the victories and challenges of every day. I invite you to develop a list of three daily affirmations to recite every morning. You will see the difference in your thinking and attitude.

Just like your emotions and thoughts, what you see also affects the five things you control (what you say, what you believe, what you think, what you feel, and what you do). The words you speak validate what you see, reflecting your interpretation of reality. Your beliefs shape your sense of truth and influence your attitudes and behaviors. Thoughts, as reflections of your beliefs, fuel the mind and spur action. They direct your intentions and decisions. Emotions and moods control thoughts and actions, guiding your responses to internal and external stimuli. Finally, your actions are a manifestation of your thoughts, feelings, beliefs, and perceptions. Those actions shape your experiences and interactions with the world around you.

All five of components are interrelated. They work in tandem to empower you through your journey of purpose.

Through my journey, I came to truly value myself. If you do not value yourself, then you will allow yourself to become a doormat in life, instead of being the door that is bold and courageous. Courage conquers fear and doubt. Do not doubt who you are. Recognize and accept your value. Look for ways to be intentional toward increasing your value. Do not become stagnant because you do not believe in what you see.

In Numbers 13, a group of twelve men were sent out to scout the new land of Canaan that was to be the Israelites'. Ten of the twelve returned with a negative report. They stated, "We seemed like grasshoppers in our own eyes, and we looked the same to them." Because of how they viewed themselves, the people were unable to moving forward. Your perception of yourself can either hinder or liberate. You will either move forward or stay stuck because of what you see.

In Numbers 13, the people looked at themselves and saw inferiority and smallness. Because of this, they wandered the desert for forty years. The majority died there, never reaching the Promised Land.

Be careful of who you allow to influence what you see. In Mark 5:37, a seemingly simple verse carries profound wisdom: "He did not let anyone follow him except Peter, James and John the brother of James." In these few words, Jesus demonstrates a powerful lesson in discernment and faith. He chooses specific individuals to witness certain events. This highlights the importance of surrounding one's self with believers and supporters who share the vision and trust in the journey ahead.

Jesus' selective approach serves as a guiding principle for your life and endeavors. Just as he carefully curated his inner circle, you too must be intentional about who you allow to accompany you on your journeys.

Here are important factors to consider as you choose your circle:

1. Quality over quantity: Jesus prioritized quality over quantity when selecting his companions. He recognized that having a few faithful and supportive individuals was far more impactful than having a multitude of followers who lacked genuine belief. It is crucial to prioritize depth of connection over

sheer numbers. Surrounding yourself with a select few who truly understand and support your vision can lead to more meaningful relationships and greater success in your endeavors.

2. Shared vision and faith: Jesus chose disciples who shared his vision and had faith in his teachings. Surround yourself with individuals who align with your goals and values and who have faith in your abilities. Having a support system of like-minded individuals who believe in what you are doing will better equip you to overcome obstacles and achieve your objectives.

3. Trust and reliability: By limiting his inner circle to a select few, Jesus fostered a sense of trust and reliability among his followers. He knew that he could depend on Peter, James, and John to support him through the trials and tribulations ahead. In your own life, cultivating relationships built on trust and reliability is essential for navigating challenges and achieving success.

4. Protection from negativity: Jesus' selective approach also served to protect his mission from negativity and doubt. By surrounding himself with believers, he created a supportive environment conducive to growth and progress. Similarly, you must be mindful of the influence that negative or unsupportive individuals can have on your journey. Surrounding yourself with positivity and encouragement can help you stay focused and motivated to pursue your goals.

Jesus' example a powerful lesson in discernment and faith. Just as Jesus carefully chose his companions, we too must be selective about who we allow to join us on our journeys. Surround yourself with others who share your vision, values, and faith—build a support system that empowers you to overcome challenges and achieve your goals. There is transformative power in surrounding yourself with those who believe in you.

For the twenty years I worked at my agency, I was seeking the approval and acceptance of my leadership and peers, which impacted how I saw myself. I had to stand firm and believe in who I was. I had to stop looking to them and instead look to God. How I define myself affects the five things that I control and the picture that I paint for my life. It affects my hope, my future, what I will pursue, what I attend, and the strength of my drive.

I was so focused on pleasing others and trying to become something I was not instead of being myself and believing in the person God created. In *The Book of Wellness,* author Donald B. Ardell states that the greatest cause of disharmony in individuals occurs when they surrender to the will of others instead of taking responsibility for their self.[9] Individuals must take personal responsibility by controlling their choices in all aspects of their lives. This allows them to lives that maximize wellness and health.

I wasted energy that should have been expended on pursuing my "why" instead of trying to fit in. Who I sought to please could not be man but God. For me to please God, I needed to accept myself. I needed to become comfortable with the skin I was in and the person within this vessel of clay. I had to learn how to truly see myself—that I was beautiful, that I was made in God's image, and that God created me as I am.

---

9 Donald B. Ardell, *The Book of Wellness: A Secular Approach to Spirit, Meaning & Purpose* (Prometheus Books, 1996).

Be happy with the person you are. Do not attempt to become something you are not to fit in with the crowd. For me, I had to return to my roots—to high school and Ms. Davis. I had to return to the values my parents instilled in me. I had to be me, as the quote goes, because everyone else is taken. There is nothing wrong with being me. I am beautiful, and I am a warrior.

Working in corporate America, seeking to climb the ladder, the roadblocks I encountered reflected the most innate parts of myself. I am a confident Black woman with a brain built to develop strategies for being the best in anything I do. I am not a follower, and I do not cower. I am respectful and confident in myself. I work within the rules to achieve my desired outcomes. I will not empower man to make me into something I am not, nor will I place him on a pedestal. I am a person of faith. I believe in the Creator. I know that his Word is true. I must be obedient and follow him. He knows the way. I must let him lead.

I recall conversations I had with supervisors who would say to me, "You have a strong personality. You need to tone down your opinions. Be more mild and gentle. You appear to be aggressive and bold." Initially I was offended by this feedback; however, I had to learn to see what was really behind the words. The truth behind these words was that I command presence. When I walk into a room, I have confidence because I believe in my value. I am a beautiful, smart Black woman. I am someone others should get to know.

Do not take this as me being prideful. I am a humble person. All that I am is because of the One who created me. He instilled in me talents and gifts so I could become the person I need to be to fulfill my purpose. It is this gift within me that challenges others, makes me stand out, and causes others to be uncomfortable. It was not my words; it was my presence that caused others to be uneasy.

I found that when my supervisors spoke these words to me, what they were really saying was, "Do not say anything, just go along. Do not have an opinion. Follow the men. Do not make any waves." But I am not a follower. I have a voice that must be heard. When I look in the mirror, I see a woman who is courageous. I am a servant. I love to connect with others and help them remove the scales that block them from seeing, allowing them to be led by the Spirit. I want them to see beyond the physical self. The Spirit allows you to see from the perspective of God. He is love, and He hopes mankind will embrace the spirit each of us has been gifted. Let the Spirit be your counselor, not your eyes nor man.

Look in the mirror. See the person you are and believe. Believe, as I am working to do each day of my life. I owe it to myself to honor the meaning of my name.

Earlier in the book, I told the story about my brother. I recall a conversation he had with my sister. He had met a woman and was looking to marry her. My sister and I had reservations. We both thought he was moving too fast and that he should wait, take some time to get to know himself, and find his direction. He had just gotten out of a bad relationship that did not bring out the best in him, and my sister and I wanted the best for him. We could see the potential and goodness in him. However, he did not see it. What he saw was that he needed another person to make him whole. My brother made his decisions based on emotions, physicality, and feelings. This was not based on the Spirit or looking within.

This new woman he met was nice. However, we did not know a lot about her and neither did he. He just went with what felt good. My sister and I said to wait.

My brother looked at my sister and asked, "Don't I deserve to be happy?"

My brother's view of happiness depended on being with another. He was not content with himself, so he sought others to bring him contentment and joy. Failing to see his own value resulted in unfruitful decisions.

My brother married his second wife against our reservations. We were not against the woman. We were against the reasons behind the marriage. It was not based on love. It was based on looking for someone to help him love himself. He saw himself as lacking. My brother had a talent. He built his entire computer from scratch. It was a masterpiece. This talent could have been used to build a business, but it never happened.

In 1 Corinthians 3, the people were concerned with who they followed: Paul or Apollo. Whoever baptized them determined who they claimed allegiance to, but their concern was misplaced. They should have been focused on the who who made them grow. It does not matter who waters and plants; what is paramount is who provides the growth. My brother thought a person provided his growth. He looked to a woman instead of looking to the One who created him, who would open his eyes to himself. He failed to travel within himself.

He did not see himself. This resulted in his demise. The world makes it easy to focus on the tangible instead of the intangible. The intangible is the Spirit, Jesus, and God. None of these we can see; however, we can feel the presence of all three. Being in their presence will allow you to get in touch with yourself. Our history is filled with individuals who were confident in themselves. Each looked in the mirror seeing their greatness. What they saw empowered them to press forward and become the person they were created to be.

For eighteen years, Nelson Mandela was imprisoned in a seven-foot by nine-foot cell. He stated that they could cage his body, but his mind could not be caged. Nelson, after serving twenty-seven years in prison, became the President of South Africa. He believed in himself. As with Mandela, we cannot allow our minds to be caged by what we see in ourselves.

I say to you: believe. Believing will empower you to see more. Each day when I wake up, I say to myself, "I believe in me. I can do what I set out to accomplish today." Have faith in yourself. See yourself, not the world. Do not allow the world to dictate and control what you see. The world seeks to stop you and hold you back. Look at the evidence—it is clear. You are amazing. Believe in you. See yourself for who you are and become what you see.

EPILOGUE

Open my eyes that I may see wonderful things in your law.

– PSALM 119:18

Unlike our physical eyesight that begins to dim with age, our spiritual sight becomes better as time progresses. The development of sight is a continual process. You change your life by changing your sight. I thought that to change my life, I had to change others. But what needed changing was me and how I looked at myself, God, and the world—not with my physical sight but with the Spirit. I am still a work in progress. My journey continues.

I am now in a new season of my life. God has blessed me with freedom to proceed to the next level, and I am committed to pressing forward to make my career a reality. I am passionate about and dedicated to reading, writing, speaking, and training. I am going to share my knowledge and skills with others to help them see beyond their physical sight. Seeing beyond physical sight is scary and uncomfortable. What you see requires you to act in faith and hope. I will continue to take leaps, believing in what can be. I will not allow the world or individuals to dictate what I can become.

There will be storms and trials that will test my faith in myself. I will not give up, and I will not turn back. I believe. I will not allow the negative thoughts to win in my mind. I am going to succeed.

The Apostle Paul says it best in Philippians 4:13: "Finally, brothers and sisters, whatever is true, whatever is noble, whatever is right, whatever is pure, whatever is lovely, whatever is admirable—if anything is excellent or praiseworthy—think about such things." It took me twenty years to learn that sight is not physical but spiritual. I focused on seeing with my eyes instead of seeing with the Spirit to find the true, noble, right, pure, lovely, and admirable. My eyes were focusing on all the opposites: what was wrong, unjust, sinful, ugly, hateful, and despicable. Focusing on these things clouded my outlook on life and people. Once I turned my focus to the good, my connection with my Source became stronger. It enabled me to see how he sees. It changed my life for the better.

Stop using physical sight as your only way to see. See with your spirit, and you will see situations and people with hope and faith.

Spirit Does Not Give Up

On most days, I take my furry baby girls for a walk, as it is our time to be together and for me to have time with the Lord. I took my girls to the trail this morning. As always, we started off running. I kept them with me, running on the leash. At the top, the trail has two small lakes: one in the center of the trail and a lake to the south of the trail. This morning, when we reached the top, I let Mercedes and Lexus off their leashes so they could stretch their legs at the top by the lake in the center.

Mercedes is a water furry baby. She adores the water. She took off to the lake with Lexus following suit. After a bit, I called them to return. Mercedes came streaking past me and headed off down the trail. No Lexus. I called for Lexus while keeping my eyes on Mercedes. Mercedes ran back towards the water. I thought she was going for Lexus, who is only three months old, to rescue her. Instead, Mercedes dove back into the water and swam over to the other side to greet a gentleman walking on the trail. I called for Mercedes to get back to me while I continued looking for Lexus.

Suddenly, Lexus came running towards me. Mercedes swam back across the lake and streaked toward me again. I turned my back momentarily, as I thought she was coming back to me. I grabbed Lexus and then turned to get Mercedes.

I lost sight of Mercedes again. I called for her, but she still didn't return to me. I started walking down the trail calling for her; still, no Mercedes. Lexus was walking with me, pulling me to run, so I ran with her. We still did not find Mercedes. About five minutes lapsed, but still no Mercedes. I returned to where I had last seen her, thinking she was in the tall brush. I continued calling for her, but she did not return. Ten minutes passed with no sign of her. I passed a fellow walker, who I see on a regular basis, and asked if he had seen my baby girl. He said no. I gave him my card to call me if he found her.

Fifteen minutes had passed, and I grew concerned. Still no Mercedes. I called my local police for assistance. They stated no one had reported seeing a yellow Labrador Retriever, but they said they would keep an eye out for her. I could not find her. I continued looking around the park, but still there was no sign of her. I said, "God, I know I am going to find her. Once I find her, she is going to be punished. Her off-leash privileges have been revoked."

At this time, about thirty minutes had passed with no Mercedes. My phone rang. It was the fellow walker on the trail telling me he had my baby girl. I knew I was going to find her. I saw with the Spirit that I was going to find her. I did not doubt it. I had hope and faith. When you see with the Spirit, you have confidence and believe.

This is how I am going to move forward into the next seasons of my life. I am a work in progress. My training in seeing is not over—it is only beginning. It will get better and stronger. I am thankful and grateful to God for opening my sight to see beyond. Do not allow your physical sight to trick you into thinking that what you dream is not possible. It is possible. Do not give up.

SEE TO TRANSFORM

As I go forward, I will look back to pause and revisit my victories. My victories will pull me through when times get tough. I will be thankful and grateful because the experiences make me better and stronger. I will be elated and overjoyed that God allowed me to have the experience. The experience adds to my character. I am being transformed by the disruptions in my life. See disruption as an opportunity to reach a new "normal" that results in higher levels of development. Development is a process that does not cease. I have joy and peace in seeing the person I am today compared to the person I was. I have joy and peace because the Father is with me.

I know I must continually strive for better. There is so much within me still waiting to be unleashed. I am not finished. I will not be done until death. I will keep soaring, seeking higher ground.

Joshua was fearful to take on the task of becoming a leader, but God created him to be a leader. In Joshua 1:9, God said to him, "Be strong and courageous. Do not be afraid; do not be discouraged, for the Lord your God will be with you wherever you go." As God was with Joshua, he is with you and me. We will continue to soar higher as our sight gets better. Do not be afraid to become your best self.

You have the authority and tenacity to become the person you were destined to be if you commit to being so. Isaiah 40:31 states, "but those who hope in the Lord will renew their strength. They will soar on wings like eagles; they run and not grow weary, they will walk and not be faint." This can be you: you can have endurance in the journey of growth and see sustainable progress rather than temporary change. You are the only person stopping yourself from soaring to new levels in your life.

You owe it to yourself to open your mind and see beyond what others see for you. Do not allow the world or people to dictate who you can become. Do not allow the world or people to control your mind. Open your mind so that you will see with your spiritual eyes. If you allow your vision to be clouded and controlled by others, you will miss out on seeing the opportunities in your life. You have a vision that can be realized and achieved.

Life is to be lived to the fullest. To live to the fullest, you must transform how you think and see. You will not progress if you do not open your mind. I look back over my life and I see that without changing how I viewed my experiences, people, and situations, I would not be the person I am today. Without opening my eyes, I would have been stymied in my growth and development. I would not be the author of four books, including this one, and I would not have founded my two companies, Faith Hope & Spirit LLC and Ava's Pathways. Instead, I would have worked a job in which I was miserable, living a life that was below average. I would be dreading the weekdays, rushing for the weekend to arrive so I could get a temporary reprieve from the prison I had created. I would have wasted my potential and gifts, leaving them still wrapped and untapped.

Life is precious and is not to be wasted. Each day is a blessing that is not to be squandered. Each of us is exceptional. You must realize and believe in the greatness that is within. Believing is the biggest hurdle you will face. Once you believe, the rest will follow. You will realize that nothing is impossible for you to do. You will have broken down the barriers that you have placed in your mind, barriers that hold you back. You were created for a purpose. It is up to you to find and pursue that purpose.

Look at all of those who have gone before us and those who are still paving the way. They pave the way because they believe. They faced hurdles, obstacles, pain, and hardship; however, all kept pressing forward. They did not allow their minds to become closed. Martin Luther King, Jr. fathered the civil rights movement. Oprah Winfrey broke down the barriers for women of color in TV talk shows. Hillary Rodham Clinton showed that a woman can run for president. Kamala Harris was elected to be the first African American Vice President of the U.S.. Colonel Sanders, at the age of sixty three, founded KFC. Debbie Fields founded a multi-million dollar corporation from one cookie recipe. Virginia Walden Ford fought for her son to receive a better education by spearheading the DC Opportunity Scholarship Program that helps underprivileged children access high-caliber schools. Nelson Mandela, imprisoned for twenty-seven years, eighteen of which were in a seven-by-nine-foot cell, still became the first Black South African President and ended apartheid in his country. These are just a few examples. There are so many more who are paving the way because they saw beyond their physical sight. They saw with their spirit. They did not allow the world to dictate who and what they could become. They saw and believed because of their hope in the unseen.

Do not settle for seeing people like trees, like the man in Mark 8:24. His sight was being restored, but he could still only see in part. Jesus laid his hands on the man's eyes again. When he took another look, he saw clearly for the first time. Take another look so you can see and realize what can be. The fuzzy shapes will become clear. Look beyond to see not with just your eyes but with the Spirit.

QUESTIONS FOR REFLECTION

1. What systems were instrumental in your childhood?
2. What were the impacts of the systems in your childhood on forming your identity?
3. What are the top five values of the culture you were raised in?
4. What are your top five values?
5. How do your values shape your identity? Be specific.
6. What are your top three strengths?
7. How your strengths shape your identity? Be specific.
8. Summarize your purpose in two to three sentences. Incorporate your values, strengths, and identity.
9. What impact does your identity have on your purpose?
10. What are the biggest lessons you have learned in your career or life so far?

11. How have these lessons impacted your identity? Be specific.
12. How have you applied these lessons to move forward?
13. What destinations do you have in mind for the journey of your life? Incorporate what you see with the Spirit.
14. What are your goals for reaching the destinations?
15. Develop a plan of action along with steps for reaching those goals.
16. Find an accountability partner to aid in keeping you on track to reach your destinations.
17. What role does faith play in your life?
18. In what ways has unbelief held you back?
19. What is your strategy for conquering unbelief?
20. Where is your quiet place?
21. How are you incorporating your quiet place into your life?
22. In what ways can you make your quiet place an integral part of your life?
23. How are you using your quiet space to cultivate your spiritual sight?
24. Who are the individuals in your circle?
25. In what ways do they sharpen you?
26. What is the metaphorical mountain in your life—the place you struggle to move on from?
27. What will it take for you to leave the mountain?
28. Identify actions you can take over the next thirty, sixty, and

ninety days. Rinse and repeat this process until you leave the mountain.

29. What lessons have you learned from your deserts?
30. What are five soundtracks that play in your mind?
31. What impact do these soundtracks have on your thinking and actions?
32. How can you replace these with soundtracks that activate you and your purpose?
33. Define what it means to live your life with no limits, seeing beyond your physical sight.
34. Describe the vision you see.
35. What actions do you need to take to make the vision visible?
36. Set thirty, sixty, and ninety-day goals to achieve the actions.
37. Evaluate your progress every thirty days and adjust your goals as needed.

www.ingramcontent.com/pod-product-compliance
Lightning Source LLC
Chambersburg PA
CBHW071707090426
42738CB00009B/1698